D0426587

119982023

THE BUSINESS COACH

THE
BUSINESS
COACH

A Game Plan for the
New Work Environment

JAMES S. DOYLE

John Wiley & Sons, Inc.
New York • Chichester • Weinheim • Brisbane • Singapore • Toronto

This book is printed on acid-free paper. ∞

Copyright © 1999 by James S. Doyle. All rights reserved.

Published by John Wiley & Sons, Inc.

Published simultaneously in Canada.

Designations used by companies to distinguish their products are often claimed by trademarks. In all instances where the author or publisher is aware of a claim, the product names appear in Initial Capital letters. Readers, however, should contact the appropriate companies for more complete information regarding trademarks and registration.

This publication is designed to provide accurate and authoritative information in regard to the subject matter covered. It is sold with the understanding that the publisher is not engaged in rendering legal, accounting, or other professional services. If legal advice or other expert assistance is required, the services of a competent professional person should be sought.

Library of Congress Cataloging-in-Publication Data:

Doyle, James S.
    The business coach : a game plan for the new work environment /
James S. Doyle.
        p.   cm.
    Includes bibliographical references and index.
    ISBN 0-471-29326-1 (cloth : alk. paper)
    1. Executives—Training of.   2. Executive ability.   I. Title.
HD30.4.D68   1999
648.4'07124—dc21   98-35144

Printed in the United States of America.

10 9 8 7 6 5 4 3 2 1

To my family,
For their inspiration to be a great coach.
I dedicate this book to Vicki and my sons Jim,
Ryan, Sean, Blake, Connor.

Contents

Preface: Training Camp for Senior Executives

Becoming a Coach

For over 100 years this giant international company had staked its claim as being a world-class organization. The CEO/chairman was a man of vision and he was more of an international statesman than a business executive. He had built a coalition of political, geographical, and economic leaders to provide a base for customer distribution channels and business opportunities.

The company had grown from modest beginnings to become a diversified and powerful multinational firm. Its tentacles reached around the globe to all continents, and there were many growth projections for new markets in still more locations in the world.

The firm's name was its greatest asset. Integrity was key to its name, being honored as second to none. The trust this firm had established with its customers stood untarnished in the global marketplace. Its corporate citizenship around the world was held in highest esteem and was the envy of both large and small competitors. There was no doubt that this huge conglomerate was at the top of its business game.

Many of the company's old-guard management couldn't see the need for change. For them life appeared to be a calm and placid body of water. Many of these executives viewed the world and themselves as market leaders. Still others believed that strong traditions and values should be preserved and left untouched. "After all, we should stick with what got us here," their logic would say. "We are comfortable and secure, and we know what works."

Financial returns seemed to support their way of thinking. They found solace in the employee data that said our employees were basically satisfied; turnover was low. Customers seemed satisfied as well. "So, we are in good shape," said the old guard. Further evidence that life was grand came with back-to-back record years of earnings.

Yet the CEO/chairman knew better. Things were calm on the surface, but he saw potential turbulence developing on the horizon, as the company prepared itself for the next generation of managers. A new guard taking over the helm of a massive corporate vessel always causes turbulence.

The chairman saw a need to anticipate and ensure safe passage by charting the uncertain and often turbulent seas of competition and by guiding the firm through a fundamental change of leadership and leadership style. Coaching was the new leadership style that he saw as keeping the firm On Top of its game—and that's where he wanted to keep the firm positioned.

At the chairman's request a group of the company's senior worldwide leaders gathered at a retreat to explore what it would mean to *become coaches* and be less invested in the old top-down style of management. This voyage of discovery and exploration would prove to be a pivotal move in the total renovation of the firm. The strategic initiatives that came out of this retreat were critical. The session on "Becoming a Coach" launched a new way of thinking about the critical managerial competencies needed for the future success of the firm.

Imagine for a minute a real-life scene at this retreat:

The attendees were gathered around the coffee station engaged in conversation and "executive-speak" associated with worldwide executives of their stature. Warm-up dialogue quickly gave way to specific questions in their bantering:

"Do you suppose he [the CEO/chairman] really expects us to act like coaches?"

"Yeah, does he expect us to reincarnate as Vince Lombardi—or, better yet, be like Bobby Knight?"

Grabbing a muffin and a refill of coffee, the three dozen attendees took their seats and "acted executive," or cool and above it all. The moderator began, "Welcome, everyone. Who would like to tell this distinguished group of world business leaders what it means to truly 'Be a coach'?"

Their coolness translated to "Don't make the first move. Lie back and check out the political correctness of our answers." After a moment of unresponsiveness the moderator suggested how long a day it would be if no one spoke up. Suddenly the room exploded with an automatic weapon fire of responses, including the following and more.

A coach . . .

• Is a leader.	• Teaches.
• Is a good listener.	• Supports.
• Is results-oriented.	• Is a winner.
• Is a role model.	• Is a pacesetter.
• Has high standards.	• Inspires high performance.
• Is focused.	• Is trusted.
• Is respected.	• Is bottom line–oriented.
• Demands excellence.	• Is knowledgeable.

Can you relate to this image? The opening discussion proved lively as well as interesting as it took on a life of its own.

As the day unfolded in this initial session the executives better understood the new learning required to *be* a coach. An importance success factor was missing for all attendees. They discovered it was much easier to talk about coaching than to walk the talk of truly being a coach. They became aware that the challenge of authentic practice as a coach in business was vital and a core managerial competency—that the era of quick fixes and top-down managerial style was ending.

They also quickly discovered that in order to stay on top as a firm as new management came on board, there were critical areas of development that needed to take place. Some of these were learning to:

- *Become* coaches from the *inside out.*
- Move through *transitions* and *turbulence.*
- Understand what *new work environments* means.
- Learn how to *chalk the field* and work together creating a team.
- Use the *language of coaching* from the inside out.
- Use authentic *coaching strategies.*

They also learned this would take time, patience, and training. The banter around the coffee station seemed shallow now. They were ready to challenge themselves and their company to remain a leader through a new and proven managerial style of success—coaching! Now they now knew what it meant and what it could be.

Thus began the process of becoming a coach for this highly compensated and powerful group of business executives. They were learning how to get themselves in shape as coaches. The buy-in was deeper than the CEO could have hoped for.

How about you? Are you ready to go through a learning process with authentic practice that will enable you to be a fine-tuned business coach, creating a game plan for new work environments? Are you ready to become even more of a team player and become an authentic coach?

Acknowledgments

Winning a team championship in sports competition or creating a high-performance team in business requires the best efforts of everyone on the team. Writing a book is just the same. My life has been touched, enhanced, and enriched by many who have "coached" me through my development. I will always be grateful and appreciative of their honesty, wisdom, and support!

While I cannot name all of the workshop participants whom I have had the honor of working with and getting to know, I am grateful for their stories, input, and success as coaches.

My friend David McNally, author of *Even Eagles Need a Push*, was very supportive in the journey of writing this book.

I'm grateful to Lowell and Cay Hellervick for their coaching at a time when I needed development and competence at coaching.

Steve Cohen and his colleague Nena Backer provided much "mental toughness" in my efforts in developing the book. Jim

Collins, coauthor of *Built to Last,* and Pat Riley, one of the greatest coaches in the NBA, inspired me to think world-class.

Tom Brown encouraged me to find my agent and introduced me to John Willig, who placed the book with John Wiley & Sons.

My thanks also go to:

Rick Aberman for his encouragement and support. Tony Vlamis, whose vision brought this book to the marketplace. Andrew Stirrat for his ongoing encouragement.

Susan Reed, my friend and writing coach. Lisa Kruse, who helped with the book proposal. Carylee Kensler for her spirited editing and creativity. Lee deStefano for her diligent word-processing skills. Jack Semler, partner in Customer Inc., for his long-term view of the project and support to see it completed.

I am blessed to have friends whose encouragement and support sustained me throughout the process. I am especially thankful to and proud to know Pete Schulte, Jim and Sue Gruver, Steve and Greer Scriver, and Heidi Isaak, the ultimate cheerleader!

I am also thankful for my own family, who supported my efforts.

Finally, two men who have been coaches for me, my father-in-law Jim Halom, whose wisdom and counsel have helped me prosper in corporate life, and my father Jim Doyle.

Introduction

Life is full of interesting possibilities. What if your work environment was filled with collaboration, trust, and empowering relationships with others? What if you as a manager, peer, team member, or friend could be a real coach to others? What new possibilities might you create for your existing and new work relationships?

What is coaching? It is a planned and purposeful process. It requires a set of special skills, attitudes, and qualities. You might already be a very competent coach; perhaps you have just become inspired to learn more about coaching. Maybe your firm has adopted a coaching style of management and you are ready to learn more of what it takes to *be* a coach. No matter what your current perspective or level of competence is, *The Business Coach: A Game Plan for the New Work Environment* can help you create the necessary mind-set, skills, and attributes you need to become a coach.

It is the bold contention of this book that the greatest benefits coaches can provide those they are coaching is to see the possibilities each player, employee, or peer has that they may not see for themselves and to create a mutual game plan to attain success. When you learn this, you will be able to assist each person being coached to achieve desired goals. All great and legendary coaches leave behind a legacy of inspired and shared vision. You can be that kind of coach; it is in you already. Hold yourself as willing and able to learn the tools and practices of being a coach as outlined in this book and we will unlock the coach within you together.

The Business Coach will give you the understanding and skills, to allow transformation within you, so that you may reach a new level of competence and success as a coach in business. *The Business Coach* grew out of my experiences coaching in one of the largest multinational companies in the world, and in leading business coaching seminars in many different countries. What also inspired me to write was my profound need at times to be coached. I continue to need coaching in my life. *The Business Coach* is the game plan for everybody who wants to be a coach, and be a great one!

You will find, like I did, that there is a critical difference between *acting* like a coach and *being* one. Acting like a coach is an *outside-in* process. On the other hand, being a coach is an *inside-out* process. Learning to think and feel like a coach, is the essence of coaching. Behavior and acceptance will follow after you *become* a coach.

The Business Coach is more than a tips and techniques book. It's designed to be a highly practical guide, leading the reader through a step-by-step process of growth and mastery.

The process begins here!

1

So Who Needs a Coach?

The Business Imperative

It was spectacular outside! It was mid-November in Minnesota; the temperature was 41 degrees above zero, and the sun was brilliant against a clear blue sky. The crystalline snow glimmered like glass.

The fiscal year was half over, like halftime in a football game. The functional team was slumping; results, morale, and production were all down, and there was a negative P&L (profit and loss). The coach slumped back in his chair in despair.

He took another swallow of morning coffee, and asked himself: *Why is this department struggling? What prevents the team from performing at optimum levels? What's missing?*

He knew intellectually that he had a talented group of individuals in his department. He had worked hard on creating clarity of vision, mission, and competence, but still in his heart he could feel things weren't right.

As a manager he had inherited this assignment just a little ahead of his own competence and abilities. Across corporate America, this is more the norm than the exception, or so he thought. While no doubt in the future he would make a terrific leader, today he was far from this status.

The company wanted him to be a *coach* to those he was managing and less of a boss. As he reflected this morning on the "scorecard" of his coaching he recognized he was on the wrong side of the score! The halftime statistics on his team's performance read like those of a sports team that had left their game in the locker room and played the game as though they were two leagues below their opponents. The manager assessed his situation as frustrating.

His team was struggling with finding its purpose, its uniqueness, and the competence required to truly serve its customers. In this case the manager acting as coach knew the problem, but was blind to the possible solutions. He relied at times on his *own* strength, power, and experience, which could be either an asset or—if deployed inappropriately—a liability.

The manager had read books and attended seminars and courses in the effort to act like a coach. These learning experiences tended to be *outside-in* or worthwhile data, but, unfortunately for this coach, they were never fully internalized. Instead, the manager needed to adopt an *inside-out* approach, where his head and heart could become aligned to bring integrity, harmony, and authenticity to learning and ultimately behavior. Thinking and being should start coming together, allowing him to *be* the coach of his dreams, without the frustration.

Instead of being an authentic coach, he was a wanna-be coach—talking the talk, but failing to walk the talk. So, in the midst of this turmoil the manager studied his options.

On his desk was an invitation; as he opened it he was struck with its simplicity, and in that moment the beginning of a solution for his dilemma emerged. The inspiration came in the form of a question, *"How does this tree stay evergreen?"*

On the inside cover there was a picture of an evergreen tree on a hill. The business manager sat back, stunned by the power of the question and the essence of what it was asking. Suddenly he caught sight of a hill outside his window, a real-world picture of the one in the mailer. Sudden impact!

His mind flooded with images of seeds, growth, maturity, serenity and beauty. *Staying evergreen is not just about the luck of where seeds fall or are planted, although that helps, but about nourishment, water, environment, weather, and such.* Like a mathematical equation he put two and two together: *The creation of coaching competency is about* staying evergreen, *growing, and being a coach, not just acting like one! It's about shifting one's mindset, living, developing, and approaching relationships from an "inside-out" perspective.*

It was a wake-up call! This manager was ready to operate from an inside-out mode, ready to create a set of daily practices that would enable him to internalize the desired skills he was ready to learn. The manager had found new inspiration. Make no mistake—this was not fantasy and illusion. *I know, because I was the manager.*

At that moment I must admit I felt a bit like Scrooge, visited by several ghosts. *But I realized I was not too late; I could change, and I could learn to be an authentic coach.* The choice was mine to make!

So who needs a coach? We all do!

The pressure to perform at optimum levels in business today has never been greater. In fact, many business executives agree that the toughest job a manager has is confronting poor performance and encouraging behavior change. *Being* a coach can add to the tools you already have as a manager. As a coach you will learn how to support optimum performance and encourage successful behavior instead of poor performance.

Are you one of the managers in business today who feel overwhelmed by the rapid pace of change? And are you working longer, harder just to keep up? While attending to the daily avalanche of management responsibilities, information, and business activities, do you suddenly awaken to the fact that corporate life as you have known it is different and changed forever? The current pictorial used by management consultants for this rapid change in business is "constant white water." Are you in the rapids, too? You may be one of these managers challenged by changing work cultures. You are starting this book at the right place and right time if these perspectives apply to you.

Learning to be a great coach starts here. Great coaches have not only acquired certain knowledge, skills, and competence to coach, but they have a distinct attitude, a deep and genuine concern for the *coaching relationship*. This is true in sports, in business, and in world-class performances of all kinds.

One core competency that is getting more and more attention today in the boardroom, on the shop floor, and in regional sales offices is "coaching." This competency, if acquired and performed well, allows today's business manager to create considerable added value for the firm.

So, what is coaching? Why is it important? *"So who needs a coach?"* What makes coaching so effective? What is a coaching relationship?

Coaching in business is defined as an interactive process between managers or between a manager and an employee that enhances behavior, thought processes, and performance. Coaching involves a specialized set of learned skills when interacting with individuals and groups in the everyday workplace. Coaching is developing people on purpose. Workaday conversations between managers or between managers and employees are potentially coaching opportunities. Coaching involves employees in the process of planning, creating, and problem solving. Through coaching, a deeper understanding of points of view is developed by both the coach and the learner.

The Business Coach: A Game Plan for the New Work Environment was written to help managers like yourself in your daily activities to get more out of business relationships. However, there is a shift in thinking and behavior required of the manager in order to successfully become a coach. Embedded in coaching is the importance of *intentionality*, or the mind-set that all winning coaches have.

You may ask, "Why should I do this?"—particularly if you believe you're already a pretty good coach. And what about the company—will it support this attitude, this new way of managing?

Let's look at the first issue—the individual manager. Today, many managers believe they are overworked, overlooked, not recognized for their contributions, and underpaid. *USA Today* in April 1997 published an article in cooperation with the Ethics Officers Association about how perceived pressures at work lead to employees acting in unethical or illegal ways. The study found that 48% of respondents committed acts outside company norms, ranging from cutbacks on product quality, covering up problems, lying about sick days, lying to or deceiving customers, to putting undue pressure on coworkers. These were just a few of the 25 specific behaviors reported.

We are living at a time of unprecedented downsizing, rightsizing, reorganization, acquisition, divesting, and we are all asked to do more with less. Yet the age of technology, information, networking, and telecommunications has shrunk the world. We have been instantly brought closer to coworkers, bosses, customers, suppliers, and the competition. In many cases these advances have also added to a sense of being overwhelmed.

Often, today's managers find themselves not in the old role of functional leadership—the expert, the source of power—but more often a team leader, an influencer, a facilitator—a coach! Too often, these would-be coaches haven't received the training that would give them the skills, competencies, and attitudes to function effectively in this new role. My commitment to you is to share the skills, competencies, and attitudes that will enable you to be an even better coach.

These same issues face the collective group of individuals now called the *team*. Teams are leaner, more agile, smarter, better able to communicate, and more decisive, and respond faster to customer needs and requirements. Thus, they grab more market share, attract better people, offer better working conditions, and are just more fun to belong to!

Firms need to ward off rivals and gain competitive advantage through enhancement of employee performance and through listening to their customers. One opportunity for firms to recognize the moment and employ proven concepts of building world-class team spirit, cohesion, and optimum performance is called coaching.

The world of sports, from ancient days in Greece through today's champion Chicago Bulls, has required *coaching competence*, proving that coaching, if done well, is distinctive in its nature. Not everyone can be as good at it as one can be, if left only to natural instincts. Don Shula and Ken Blanchard point out in their collaborative book, *Everyone's a Coach* (Zondervan, 1995), and through my work, I believe they are right!

{To practice coaching well takes practice to learn the skills that bring out the best in others. The coach must acquire both the special thinking and the critical skills to excel. World-class champions all have coaches—someone who is always available to inspire them to win, to raise their level of performance beyond current requirements, and to bring them to new winning heights.

Victory is not due to the coach's play, performance, or scoring. Rather, it's the player, performing on the field, the court, or the turf who determines who wins and who loses, with the coach's support, knowing they can be their best.

It's what the coach does prior to the game, match, or event, √ and, in some cases, on the sidelines during the contest that aids the outcome. It's practice, strategy, planning, guidance, and then designing new approaches to correct deficiencies that separate success from failure. Great coaches have great competencies, which keep them distinct from wanna-bes.}

It's also true in business that coaching can help individual contributors reach new heights in performance. In business, the coach does more than coach. Most business coaches are known as managers. Thus, by definition, their job descriptions also detail a host of other activities, goals, and responsibilities. In fact, more often than not, today's business managers' job titles don't include the word "coach." However, some firms, such as Team Tires Plus, a retail service company operation in six states, do actually call their managers coaches. Regardless of whether you have the name coach in your title, you have the opportunity to *be* a coach if you choose to be one! You are already on your way to beginning your coaching training and learning about how to *be* a coach.

Clearly, there is a mystique in business about the romance of "coach." Yet, for some the sports metaphor is a turnoff, and the idea of mentor can be more appealing. The mentor performs a similar vital role to that of the coach—to listen, nurture, grow, develop talent, empower, and facilitate learning in an environment of mutual respect, trust, and accountability.

Many firms have formal mentoring programs in place today. As in coaching, the relationship must be nurtured and cared for in order for it to grow. But, there is a difference between coaching and mentoring: Coaching can happen only when requested or created by the coach, whereas mentoring can be requested or assigned. In either case, both coaching and mentoring create new possibilities for all involved. For those of you who wish to think of yourself as a mentor, you will find value as you continue reading.

Here is a perspective about *being* a coach that might enroll you in this learning process. I learned a valuable lesson about the core issues of coaching through coaching Little League baseball. All experiences can be applied to everyday life and our work environments.

It was a spectacular day for the opening of the baseball season. The smell of freshly cut grass mingled with the aroma of hot dogs and popcorn at the concession stand. The sun beamed down on the newly chalked batter's box, and the crowd buzzed with excitement as they awaited the first pitch. I jogged out to my position in left-center field, as hyped up as everybody else, and more than a little nervous. This was my first game with the team. They were counting on me. I just couldn't let them down!

And then something happened that completely changed the way I thought about that game, my work, and, ultimately, my life. An outfielder named Nick trotted by and shouted, "Hey, Coach!"

Hey, Coach! Two perfectly ordinary words from the mouth of a ten-year-old boy, and all at once I had the chills and goose bumps of one who had suddenly seen the light. *"Coach"—this guy believes I'm his coach.*

In case you've begun to wonder, I should explain that this was my debut as assistant coach for my twin sons' Little League team. As any baseball mom or dad can tell you, for the kids who play, those games are the stuff of major league hopes and dreams. Remembering the Little League games of my boyhood, it meant a lot to me as a coach, to be able to help these kids grow and develop as members of their team. But, frankly, I wasn't sure I was up to the job. Why should they accept my authority and look to me for help just because I was an adult who'd played a little baseball?

Because of bad weather, we'd had only a few practices before that opening game. But somehow, something must have convinced Nick that I deserved his confidence. He accepted me. Only when I realized that he accepted me did I really feel I *was* a coach. The uniform and clipboard didn't do it. Neither did the listing of my name as coach in the program. No—it was those two magic words from a member of the team.

That's how I came to learn one the biggest lessons of my professional life that Saturday morning among the Little Leaguers: *What makes a coach isn't titles, appearances, or tenure—it's recognition and acceptance by the team*

> I continued to be Nick's coach all season, and I worked hard to deserve the title. As the summer went on and our relationship unfolded, his trust in me grew and my interest in his progress grew as well. He turned out to be a very coachable kid. He listened carefully, took suggestions well, and worked hard. And, while he wasn't destined to be an all-star, he came a long way over the summer and contributed greatly to the team. When the season was over, he thanked me for *being* his coach. With a pat on his back and tug at my heart, I wished him luck—and thought to myself, *"Thank you for teaching me what it is to be a coach."*

I learned a couple of other basic lessons from my coaching experience that summer. The first was that I saw things in Nick's game that he couldn't, because he was so tightly focused on playing. From my perspective I was able to suggest improvements he would have been blind to, and raise his game to a level he might otherwise not have reached. Thinking over this rather obvious fact one day, I was suddenly struck by a truth I'd overlooked in all my years of coaching: *One of a coach's most important jobs is to help team members to "see."*

Over the years I've been struck by how often people are completely unaware of the holes in their game at work (I'm a prime example, as you'll discover later on). By opening their eyes to those gaps, a competent coach can help team members make specific improvements. The real value the business coach adds to the relationship is opening the way for employees to become self-aware and self-correcting. When a team has this ability, the process of improvement perpetuates itself, and performance builds continuously over the long term. The second lesson was that coaching is a two-way relationship, where the coach continually learns from the team. One of my favorite illustrations of this comes from the movie *Hoosiers.*

> Gene Hackman plays the basketball coach of tiny, rural Hickory High, which is battling the mighty Bears from South Bend Central for the Indiana state high school basketball championship. With seconds left on the clock and the game on the line, Hackman's team calls a final time-out. The team huddles, and Hackman outlines a brilliant plan using Jimmy Chipwood, their ace shooter, as a decoy. But as he talks, he senses disapproval in the players' faces. "What's the matter with you guys?" he barks. His eyes dart around the silent huddle. "What's wrong? he demands again. And then Jimmy Chipwood speaks up quietly. "I can make the shot, Coach."
>
> The coach is stunned. He had it—the one strategy that could win the game for them. But instead of being applauded for his genius, he's being challenged by his star player and the rest of the team. Time is running out. He has to make a decision: *"Do we do it my way? Or do I adjust my thinking and listen to my team?"*

Luckily for our heroes, Hollywood knows enough to listen to audiences' hearts.

Hackman changes the play, Jimmy makes the shot, and Hickory High wins the championship.

I suspect scenarios like this are played out in real-world sports and in business more often than you might think. *All great coaches are great listeners.*

As Pat Riley, coach and president of the Miami Heat, says, "If you let them, your players can inspire you."

By now you've probably gathered that sports coaching is a powerful metaphor for me in the arena of business coaching. After all, they have several things in common.

Sports and Business Coaching Parallels

• Both sports and business coaches strive to motivate, inspire, and get the extra mile from their players.

• Both demand commitment, action, and results for the team and the stakeholders that support the team.

• Both build trusting relationships with their players.

• Both need focus and vision.

• Both play to win.

But it's a big mistake to equate the two. While the domains of sports and business coaching are similar, they are also different.

It was when Nick called me "Coach" that I became one. In business the coaching relationship really begins when someone voluntarily recognizes you as having the abilities to coach. No real coaching goes on until employees decide they want coaching and that you're competent to coach. But, of course, that's not the way it works in sports. By virtue of being hired for the job, the coach is deemed competent—and it's not up to the players to agree or disagree. The coach chooses the team. It's a hierarchical, authoritarian relationship—close, yes, and cooperative to a point. But in the final analysis everyone knows who is boss.

This distinction between a great coach and a wanna-be coach is recognition by the players. This is where so many would-be business coaches get tripped up. In business, we talk about making the transition "from cop to coach." If members of a work team sense that their so-called coach is nothing more than the same old boss by a different name, the entire effort will backfire.

People come to me in complete frustration, wondering why, in spite of their best efforts to do and say the right things, their business coaching relationships have fizzled. "I just can't cut through people's cynicism and mistrust," they say to me. "What am I doing wrong?" The answer is—nothing! The problem isn't what they are doing or saying. The problem is what they are thinking. Or, even more fundamentally, what they *are*.

I've found when I work with people in coaching seminars that their biggest barrier to success is the assumption that becoming a coach is a matter of adopting certain language, behaviors, and actions—in short, mastering tips and techniques. But it's not.

The coaching relationship grows from the inside out. It is not a role you can pick up and put on like a uniform. It comes from a commitment to *be* a coach, not just a desire to act like one.

Being a coach means having the competencies and attitudes that inspire team members to *grant you authority* as their coach. Without their recognition, you're not their coach—which is why I like to bring up the story of Nick and the Little Leaguers. As with a workplace team, my authority to coach came from them. In many ways, I think those kids, perhaps more than professional athletes, set the example for coaches and teams in business. They didn't work hard because they were afraid of losing their positions. They didn't do it because they were tricked or coerced. They did it out of loyalty to their teammates, the fun of competition, the satisfaction of improving, and love for the game. Not a bad way to do business, when you think about it.

My experience with Nick and his granting me the authority to coach him parallels a similar scenario told to me in an interview with Rhonda, a vice president of procurement for a multi-billion-dollar food company.

Rhonda was a self-made executive. She was one of the few senior executives working for this food manufacturer who had risen through the plant organization. She had held production, supervisory, superintendent, and plant manager positions prior to moving to the corporate headquarters. Now, as vice president of procurement, she found herself in the paradoxical position of looking back over her 33 years in the industry with the firm, and looking forward in the twilight of her career. Rhonda wanted her legacy to be passing on her knowledge, experience, savvy, and passion for the business to her younger protégés. She found herself in a new role—adviser, mentor, and coach. But, it hadn't always been like that.

Rhonda was from the old school and had more than her share of "kick butts and take names" as part of her management heritage. But something motivated her to be different.

The process of learning and change took place within her relationship with Tina, a young, inexperienced, yet highly talented ingredient buyer. They became close when the two of them found themselves on the president's task force for restructuring the procurement function, called Project Phoenix.

Tina had both admired and feared Rhonda's reputation prior to their working together. However, as time passed, Tina sought out Rhonda's advice and counsel regularly. Rhoda then found herself in the unique position of being able to extend her own efforts through the success of Tina's. It was truly win-win for both.

Rhonda made adjustments to her driving, directive style and listened more, asked more open-ended questions, made allowances for Tina's mistakes, and encouraged her to take risks. Tina, sensing trust and mutual respect, responded even more favorably to the environment of openness, clarity of expectations, and support.

Rhonda shared with me privately that she learned as much from coaching Tina as she thought Tina had learned from her. She also said that she believed a manager's toughest job is telling direct reports that they are not performing, and she saw coaching as a key capability a manager must learn to do well.

Rhonda went on to say, "Employees today won't accept or respond to management practices of yesterday."

This is not just about managing Generation X in the workplace; rather, it's about tapping into the inner power and resources that reside inside all people, regardless of gender, race, or age. Coaching in business is good business! But, coaching takes time and patience. Many managers have little patience for corrective action when it comes to coaching. Where do you see yourself on this issue? Often managers want results or fixed problems. More and more managers are pressed for time, and it is just plain harder to get everything done in a normal workday. How do you slow down and take the time to listen?

Imagine the busy executive returning from two weeks of vacation to find 65 e-mails, numerous voice mails, direct reports flying all over the world, the new budget packet on his or her desk, and a new directive to be a "coach" arising out of the boss's recent executive off-site meeting.

No wonder companies have had so many false starts at fostering a coaching environment at work. False starts occur out of good intentions, but without follow-up to solidify coaching initiative they become only "the flavor of the month."

In this book, we'll work together to build your coaching competencies, and create a climate where successful business coaching can take place.

The Application Exercises at the end of each chapter offer invaluable practice and awareness raising. They will provide long-lasting tools that can assist you in the application of new learning. These exercises allow you to consider deeply the ideas you just gained in the previous chapter and chapters. I am offering you a unique way to translate your creative ideas from the text of this book into the real world of your business, at a pace that makes sense. These are win-win exercises; there are no wrong answers. The key words are "appropriate" or "best" circumstances, issues, objectives; and people you will be coaching.

The Application Exercises will be helpful to you while learning new coaching competencies. It's very important for you to apply yourself wholeheartedly to these activities. When you can take your time and consider your answers carefully you will reap the rewards. The more thoughtful and frank you are, the better you'll understand your strengths and weaknesses and the more successful the work we do together will be.

The win-win scenarios I have constructed offer proven concepts as well as coaching and learning opportunities for each of you. You will raise your awareness in the act of being yourself. Together, we will create new foundations of experience. You can create new options and possibilities for future real-life situations. It's time to get your journal ready and start practicing, learning, and internalizing.

As we come to the end of Chapter 1 you now have new perspectives on the powerful and influential role a coach can play in business. *So who needs a coach? Anyone who desires to improve performance and take the time to go to the next level.*

Coaching Journal

One of your key tools in developing as a coach will be careful observation—of yourself and others in coaching roles. For that purpose, it's extremely valuable to keep a coaching journal, using a simple observation form. Begin this process by recording any coaching situations you observe over the next week, paying close attention to how both the coach and the person being coached behave, and what you learn from their exchange. Use these titles in your journal:

- Coaching Situation.
- Coach.
- Person Being Coached.
- Observations.
- Lessons I Have Learned.

A Coach's Qualities

Think of a person in your life whom you would call a good coach. Name the person and list five of that person's most striking qualities or characteristics in your journal.

Name _____

1.

2.

3.

4.

5.

A Coach's Competencies

Think of a successful coach. List five of the most important skills, competencies, and areas of expertise this person has.

Name _____

1.

2.

3.

4.

5.

A Coach's Mind-Set

Refer to your answers for the first two exercises. Think about how the coach's qualities and competencies relate. Now, put coaching qualities in the left column and corresponding competencies in the right, with a column in the middle for mind-sets. How might they come together to produce a specific mind-set? For example, you might say that a characteristic of a good coach is "sincerity" and that a corresponding competency is "good listening skills." The mind-set this suggests could be "having a genuine interest in the other person's ideas."

Qualities	Mind-Sets	Competencies
1.		
2.		
3.		
4.		
5.		

SELF-INVENTORY #1

Again referring to your answers to the previous exercise, rate yourself on the qualities and competencies you've identified. Which areas are you strong in now? Which would you like to cultivate?

Strong Areas   **Areas to Cultivate**

   1.

   2.

   3.

   4.

   5.

I heard Zig Ziglar, the great speaker and motivator, say, "Success is measured not by what you've done compared to others, but by what you are capable of doing."

The exercises you have just completed will increase your capabilities as a coach by helping you make the shift to an inside-out mind-set. As you gain awareness of the qualities, skills, and behaviors of successful coaches, you are taking a crucial first step toward reinventing your own coaching relationships.

2

The Transition Game

Making the Shift to Being a Coach

This chapter will help the reader better understand the importance of adopting a more collaborative coaching mind-set, with appropriate behaviors and competencies that support the transition from manager to coach.

As a kid growing up, I remember going to the movies on Saturday afternoon and how much fun it was. My favorite films were the horror movies. In those days you could be scared by Frankenstein, Dracula, the Wolf Man, and the Mummy.

The transformation that a business manager must make to truly *be* a coach is not unlike the metamorphosis Lon Chaney Jr. would go through on-screen as the Wolf Man. Obviously, I am not advocating business executives turn into werewolves, although I am not so sure there aren't already a few out there if you view how they deal interpersonally with those around them!

Making the shift to *being* a coach is a slow, subtle, visual and behavioral change from one way of being to another. It's interesting that even with all the breakthroughs in technology and filmmaking today, John Landis in creating Michael Jackson's *Thriller* couldn't rush the process. The werewolf appearance took time to create and master.

So it is with wanna-be business managers acting like coaches learning how to transform into authentic coaches: The process of change and growth takes time.

At the end of Chapter 1 you completed Application Exercises that caused you to think about the critical skills, thinking, and behaviors necessary to function effectively as a coach. I have found in my research on coaching and the hands-on application of learning in corporations that there are different interpretations of coaching.

In workshops, I have attendees reflect on Application Exercises like you just worked on. Their responses to those questions began to help shape an important pattern for me as I framed the context of *The Business Coach*.

Asking what elements must be present in a great coach and describing what you think makes a great coach, as well as who have been coaches in your life and what made them that way, help to open your eyes to a new perspective. Participants would list two kinds of responses. One set of responses focused on qualities, attributes, and characteristics of a coach ("They were concerned about me; they made me feel that I was special; I really mattered to them"). The other set of responses tended to be skills, abilities, competencies ("They listened and communicated effectively with me").

The most common responses to each category have been:

Skills/Behaviors

- Asks questions.
- Clearly defines goals.
- Helps set priorities.
- Is an excellent communicator.
- Listens.

(continued)

Skills/Behaviors (*continued*)

- Teaches.
- Establishes ground rules.
- Takes time for me.
- Is direct.
- Builds relationships.
- Gives regular feedback.
- Delegates.
- Shares information.
- Is knowledgeable.
- Follows through.

Qualities/Attributes

- Adaptable.
- Flexible.
- Caring.
- Credible.
- Fair.
- Objective.
- Honest.
- Trustworthy.
- Open-minded.
- Vulnerable.
- Positive.
- Sensitive.
- Friendly.
- Supportive.
- Confident.
- Ethical.

Qualities/Attributes (*continued*)

- Encouraging.
- Genuine.
- Consistent.
- Organizing.
- Visible.
- Professional.
- Relaxed, able to have fun.
- Energetic.
- Constructive.
- Respectful.
- Competent as a coach.
- Interested in me.
- Dependable.
- Reliable.
- Truthful.
- Concerned.
- Has integrity.
- Demonstrates leadership.
- Understands me.
- Is a problem solver.
- Is patient.
- Manages time well.
- Walks the talk.
- Influences versus controls.

The more I listened and probed deeper into the responses the more sensitive I became to the subtle differences and interpretations of what workers think makes for effective coaches in business. Along with this insight came the awareness of the gaps that exist between what workers desire and what managers or supervisors are currently offering in the form of coaching. Workers want managers to exhibit coaching skills and behaviors to help them enhance performance.

Recognize, too, that when I speak of workers I am including high-level executives in this group, as well as employees who have spoken about their leaders and the need for coaching. Make no mistake; coaching in business is not job, class- or salary-bound. Research and real-world experience validate the need for both coaching and continuous learning to improve coaching competencies at all levels in the organization. Do you see this in your work environment?

Do you have a deeper understanding of the differences between the qualities and attributes of a coach and the skills, competencies, and behaviors that are inherent in coaches? To the untrained eye it is easy to blend these components together. Yet they are distinct and equally important in learning to be a coach. The diagram in Figure 2-1 illustrates the different types of responses and the linkage between the two by the circle labeled "Intentionality," the bonding agent of the three domains of coaching.

Intentionality is the total mind-set that coaches create for

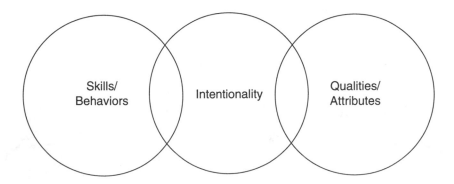

Figure 2-1 *Coaching mind-set.*

themselves about coaching and then apply to the coaching situation. This domain of coaching is important as the bonding agent for the domain of qualities, traits, and attributes and the domain of behaviors, skills, and competencies.

I have always been interested in conversations with senior managers who would express their belief that a particular manager viewed as having the "softer" skills of management, such as the attributes and traits of a coach, would not be able to have "tough" conversations with people. Often these senior managers thought of such managers as "nice guys," but unable to convey enough urgency needed to be "kick-butt." By the same token, I often heard an example of a line manager or department head who had just attended the latest corporate seminar on coaching and was now running around trying to *be* a coach. What was also reported about this type of manager was that a laminated card containing prescribed steps for coaching was used as part of the course. When managers used this card they were often perceived as unbelievable or fraudulent, because they had not shifted from the inside out.

What became obvious for me in the above examples was the disconnect between head and heart. I mean that one can attend the best seminars, read all the management books, and get the head stuff, but not feel it in the heart. The reverse is also true: One can have a big heart and not confront when it is correct to do so.

The transition game is becoming a coach with head and heart connected. This perspective caused me to look for a connector of the two domains of coaching, and as a result I created the diagram. You have seen in the diagram a visual model for the full range of coaching competence.

This connection of these three domains of coaching allows for continuity and consistency inside the coaching relationship. The coach is not seen as a manipulator seeking out an agenda or needs nor as unwilling to be up-front and honest in direct communication while coaching.

These ideas have been confirmed in my experience of presenting these concepts in workshops and one-on-one coaching situations. You need to balance the appropriate coaching skills and qualities through intentionality as a coach with your head and heart.

The following insights from manager and Hall of Famer Tommy Lasorda help illustrate the delicate balance of coaching skills.

> *Managing is like holding a dove. Squeeze too tight and you will kill it. Open your hand too much and you will let it go. That's the way it is with players.*

We have found, when working with people in coaching seminars, that their biggest barrier to success is the assumption that becoming a coach is a matter of adopting certain language, behaviors, and actions—in short, mastering tips and techniques. But this approach misses the deeper and more fundamental change that must take place: Optimum coaching ability grows from the inside out. It's not a role that can be picked up and put on like a uniform. It comes from commitment to *being* a coach, not just the desire to act like one.

Being a coach means having the competence and the attitude that inspire team members *to grant you the authority to coach them*. Without their recognition, you are not the coach. The lesson learned from coaching Nick in Little League helped me realize that.

In business today, the idea of the coach has become the role model of choice for many managers in a variety of organizations. As the game of business has been evolving and changing at a record pace, the competitive playing field has had its terrain altered as well. Organizations have become leaner, more fluid, smarter, and more responsive to the ever-changing needs of the customer. At the same time, the realities of doing business in the late 20th century have truly witnessed the reinventing of corporate America's big and small organizations.

Be it under the banner of downsizing, reengineering, rightsizing, or just plain old taking cost out of the system, in recent years firms have experienced more change and turbulence than ever before. The work world in which we now live is under siege to perform at the highest standard possible, at all times, in order to satisfy the unquenchable thirst of stakeholder value. Companies will continue to search for new and better ways to compete.

Ideas like Activity Value Analysis from McKinsey & Company and the Balanced Scorecard, which Robert S. Kaplan and David P. Norton wrote about in the January 1992 issue of *Harvard Business Review*, are tools and processes to assist in the measurement of performance against the standard. There are many leading consulting firms who stand ready and able to join forces with their clients in this epic campaign to remain competitive in the marketplace. My mission here is to illustrate ongoing organizational need for inside-out thinking about the world of work.

The ripple effect of this changing corporate landscape is that relationships at work have to be reinvented. This means competition and playing politics are not as important as building lasting relationships. Cooperation and trust building are more in favor as core skills for managers. I am not of course saying that there will never again be a political implication to the wide range of moves available to the corporate executive.

However, study after study done by organizations such as the Center for Creative Leadership, the American Society for Training and Development, Dale Carnegie, and others point out that the number one derailer of promising management careers is a fundamental inability to get along with and influence others.

The Business Coach was written to assist you as managers, team leaders, executives, or business coaches working inside organizations. We are developing a game plan for you to be more efficient, thrive, and succeed in new work environments as a coach.

I remember sitting down with a senior executive and discussing the fact that his division was having difficulty keeping a sense of shared vision, common purpose, and team. As I interviewed managers in his business, they often spoke of being overwhelmed all the time. There were constant breakdowns in relationships. Commitments were not always kept, and promises were made but broken. I was amazed at how hard these managers were working at building trusting relationships with one another, yet how frustrated they were in that effort. This could have been a natural process. After all, as human beings, being in relationships helps satisfy many of our basic needs! Yet, when I ventured the possibility of solving some of the conflict in the business by operating as a coach, I didn't fare very well with these managers on the interest meter. Why? Because the line managers couldn't see the possibilities of coaching in business and how it could help them dehassle their lives.

As it turns out, we did, over time, successfully install a coaching culture into the business, but not without significant change and reinforcement. Looking back, I discovered it didn't have to be that way. As a matter of fact, managers can learn a variety of practices that allow them to get fully engaged with those people who play significant roles in their work lives. The encouraging news is that this process of learning can be acquired by all those who are willing to hold themselves able to learn and become accountable for their behaviors. George Leonard, in his book *Mastery*, explains:

> *Mastery isn't reserved for the super talented or even for those who are fortunate enough to have gotten an early start. It's available to anyone who is willing to get on the path and stay on it, regardless of age, sex or previous experience!*

The central question here, of learning to be a coach, has two parts: First, *what is it that prevents or blocks the flourishing of deep, trusting relationships in business?* Remember that I am speaking here of those with customers, peers, subordinates, or even bosses. I am referring to the basic day-to-day interactions that drive business. These, of course, include boss-subordinate, peer-to-peer, teammate-to-teammate, between task force members, and the many other combinations that drape the corporate stage. I am also including the kind of open, trusting relationship that invites coaching.

The second critical question is, *what are the competencies that allow for authentic coaching at work?*

Earlier, I alluded to how the romance of sports coaching seduces the business executive today. And the seduction is fueled by those like me, who continue to tempt the reader with delightful tidbits of successful coaching in sports, whose actions were mimicked by their contemporaries in business. The metaphor is powerful for me and I guard its use with appropriate application. However, there are many other examples of coaching from many walks of life.

Perhaps you have seen, on television or in newspapers, responses by coaches to reporters asking something like, "Hey, Coach, would you tell me what the most important fact of coaching was for you in your career as a coach?" On many occasions the sports coach responds in rather quick yet heartfelt emotion and words: "It was how well I got to know and appreciate my players."

Bud Grant, former coach of the Minnesota Vikings and a member of professional football's Hall of Fame, said the following upon reflecting about his success:

> As a coach, you don't get here because you can kick or catch or tackle or run or throw. You get here because you have the help of a lot of people. You reflect on what a lot of people have done.

Many other coaches have said similar statements about their success.

In the next chapter, we will discuss the differences between managing and coaching, but here is a brief sneak preview. One definition (which reinforces the coaching theme) is that *managing is getting things done through others.* Sound familiar? In many firms today, this definition is the preferred one, but what gets played out and rewarded is a more direct, telling style of managing.

The reason I raise this issue is to illustrate the difficulty many

managers have in performing what may well be the toughest responsibility of their job, confronting poor performance. This annual conversation has led to significant "trust-busting" and
breakdown of the relationships in business as well.

Based on my own experience, as well as that of others, regarding giving and receiving performance discussions, I
thought of a unique way to illustrate the balanced application of
skills and attributes of the coach (as seen earlier in Figure 2-1).
The concept comes out of a tradition of excellence and world-
class performance. In thinking about the bonding together of
the qualities and competence of the coach, I again was con-
stantly inspired and humbled by the real-world case histories of
those who participated in workshops, focus groups, surveys,
and one-on-one interviews.

> Often I was told of a coach—the high school drama teacher who
> would bring out the best in a young, rising student actor, the chem-
> istry professor whose extra time and patience paid great dividends
> in the learning of a would-be chemist. I heard examples from the
> trades—the master craftsman who painfully taught his skill to his
> apprentice—and heard about the piano teacher whose pupil would
> rather be outside playing with friends, yet the teacher made the les-
> son fun and the time flew by!

These are the kinds of examples that put a lump in your
throat and make you want to relive those moments of pride and
perseverance in learning. There was never any difficulty in
hearing of the accomplishment of a coach and a learner, but
there was also, unfortunately, the perspective of incompetent,
amateur coaching.

I am not speaking of nonprofessionals here, but rather of
those coaches who pretend to possess knowledge and skill,
and instead are shallow in competence or hollow inside their
very being.

Thus, I also bore witness to stories of the coach in business
who, upon edict from corporate headquarters, attended the latest offering in courses and was now pronounced fit to coach.

These wanna-be coaches are often referred to by field people as "legends in their own minds."

Another wanna-be business coach is the "do-gooder." This variety of coach has the kindest, gentlest soul that one could ever want. The problem is that they are often taken advantage of, and they have a very difficult time handling conflict.

As I mentioned earlier, I was struck with the paradox of a coach needing to be skilled and competent, while at the same time the skills must be balanced with the qualities and characteristics of a coach.

The transition I am leading up to is balance. *I recognized the balance of mind and heart in coaching. Being* the coach is more than just acting like one.

How do you get a handle on it? Most critical to authentic coaching in business is what I call *intentionality*, or the mind-set the coach brings to the coaching relationship. In an alliance with Nena Backer of the Learning Design Group, we cocreated a self-assessment tool. This tool could be valuable in giving a manager a sense of his or her current thinking and behavior as a coach. In addition, it offers a view of how others see an individual in the role as coach. Obviously, there is a multitude of excellent tools, assessments, and instruments available for managers and executives to use in coaching today. Ours is one of many and was designed primarily as a way for a manager or peer turned coach to have an objective conversation with those close to him or her, in order to improve coaching competence, confidence, or attitude.

The examples in the Application Exercises are the questionnaires both for the coach and for others who will be offering feedback about the coach at a group session.

The intentionality tool, as we developed it, includes the values, underlying beliefs, and feelings about coaching that form the basis for trust and openness in the coaching relationship. We found that this set of questions caused attendees to think more deeply about their beliefs and behaviors with regard to the coaching relationship. When coaches compare their beliefs about coaching with those of people they are a coaching, very interesting insights occur.

In this process you would follow outlined steps and do a complete self-assessment. You would then choose three to five of your direct reports, peers, colleagues, or team members who would be in a position to answer the "Other's Assessment" questionnaire and honestly give feedback to you. This learning design is geared to open up the conversation between you as a coach and your coachee. Collect and analyze your own data prior to reading the next chapter.

The Intentional Coach Analysis of Results form appears in the Application Exercises at the end of this chapter. Notice how in this individual learning process you have gained insights from this exercise. It has enabled you to acquire new perspectives on your intentionality as a coach. How will these insights impact the coaching relationships you have or are developing?

The key to learning from this tool is that a shift can occur in the mind of the manager/coach. It's not enough to merely put on the coach's uniform and act like a coach. For if today's manager in the business or professional world pretends to *be* a coach but continues to act like a boss, the manager creates distance and mistrust inside the coaching relationship.

The following real-life examples of business professionals as they reacted to their feedback from those they were coaching support the power of their intentionality as a coach.

> Dan and Nancy were on opposite ends of the managerial style continuum. Dan was an easygoing, amiable type of manager. He really enjoyed relationships with people. Others would describe him as friendly, likable, relaxed, and easy to get along with. Dan had been a manager for eight years, and had proven himself through a variety of assignments both in the field and at headquarters.
>
> Nancy was a terrific manager. She was a very well-organized, professional, highly knowledgeable, take-charge professional. Nancy, more often than not, acted as if there was a sense of urgency to the tasks she was engaged in. Others would describe her as businesslike and having a no-nonsense approach to taking care of business.

What was interesting to me was that given their differences in persona, their reactions when given feedback about coaching others were remarkably similar. Since they were so different in dealing with people, their scores on the tally sheets reflected those differences as well. For our purposes, knowing each of their ratings is not as important as learning from their reactions and the behaviors that followed.

You will recall that the first step in the assessment process is for the participants to self-score their responses on how they see themselves as a coach and rate certain beliefs about coaching. We also asked the participants to be honest with themselves; after all, why cheat yourself? The second component then is the input of others as they experience the person as a coach. Now, while this is subtle, you will notice I said "the person," not "your manager," because in many cases the attendee is soliciting feedback from peers and bosses. Next, the coach gains a complete picture of what's going on by charting out and analyzing his or her tally sheets and coming prepared to discuss them. It is here that the similarities between Dan and Nancy began to display themselves.

As Dan and Nancy each expressed their reactions to the data, each struggled to accept the feedback from those whom they had asked for input. Notice how each of these managers reacted to the feedback they received from those they were trying to coach.

Dan had been operating under the belief that he was close to his team, that he made clear decisions, while valuing the relationships he had with people.

Dan was crushed by the fact that others saw him as wishy-washy and prone to acquiesce under pressure and conflict. While he was thought of as friendly, conservative, easygoing and people-oriented, he tended to avoid giving direct feedback and having the "direct conversation." Point numbers 8, 9, and 10 produced gaps in his own assessment of how he was performing with others as a coach. (The numbers will make more sense to you later.)

Nancy, on the other hand, had a more controlling response to the gaps between her own assessment and that of others. They were simply wrong! Nancy's ability to lead, direct, and be thorough and efficient were never questioned. Points 4, 6, 10, and 11 produced much concern for Nancy. She believed a take-charge, direct, highly assertive approach makes the best coach. While she gave consistent, regular feedback to those she coached, she lacked the interpersonal skills to recognize that people are different and a coach must be flexible and willing to act in ways that are conducive to connecting with others. Nancy was blind to what her team really expected from her. Her team members were each unique and different.

Nancy tended to approach every situation in a calm, logical, self-controlled manner, when at times being more spontaneous, relaxed, emotional, and friendly would have been more appropriate and would have closed the gap in the area of personal involvement and given her a sense of collaboration with others.

This approach would have been more appropriate given differences in people's styles of behavior. Both Dan and Nancy acted defensively and reacted negatively to the feedback they received from others. Great coaches learn much from those they are coaching, if they remain open to learning. Remember, we are less concerned with what is right or wrong than with how one can better connect, dialogue and, work with others. The coach, upon seeing the possibility to connect with others, recognizes the need to make shifts in his or her own thinking and behavior to more effectively coach others.

Thanks to my friends at the Learning Design Group, specifically Nena Backer and Steve Cohen, we created the Intentional Coach Inventory, a tool for you to apply as a way to further identify your coaching effectiveness and gain feedback from those you are coaching. You may be thinking, "Gee, do I really want to know what others think about me as a coach? Do I want to be that vulnerable, to open myself up to critique, feedback? And what do I do once I know how they feel?"

These are very legitimate questions and ones you will need to answer for yourself. The only true way to learn of our potential blind spots is to gain the insights from others. If you follow that guideline and approach this learning honestly and openly, I believe you will find others will, too, and will help you learn. You may choose to assess yourself first, think about your responses, and then ask others for their input.

Where are you in your transition to becoming a better coach? Perhaps now you have created new options and alternatives for yourself as you move toward *being* a highly competent coach.

INTENTIONAL COACH—SELF-INVENTORY #2*

Circle the response to the following statements that reflects your current belief. Be completely honest.

Response Choices

(R) Rarely	I rarely feel or think this way. In fact, most of the time the opposite is true.
(S) Sometimes	Infrequently, I may believe and/or act in this way, depending on the situation and the person.
(F) Frequently	This represents my honest beliefs in most situations with most people; there are, however, times and situations when I don't act/feel this way.
(A) Almost always	This is deeply rooted in my belief and value system and influences my thoughts and actions directly and consistently.

I Believe That   Rating

1. People in the workplace have unlimited   R S F A
   capabilities; learning, growth, and
   change are always possible.

2. Job position or title does not ensure one   R S F A
   person to have power or authority over
   others.

3. Healthy, positive, trusting relationships   R S F A
   directly contribute to producing better
   business results.

*Developed with the Learning Design Group.

4. Collaboration produces better results than individual efforts. R S F A

5. People in the workplace want to improve, make contributions. R S F A

6. Mistakes or errors can be opportunities for learning, not just punishment. R S F A

7. The coach can learn as much as the person being coached. R S F A

8. People need frequent, honest, consistent feedback on what's going well and what needs to be improved. R S F A

9. Effective, frequent coaching of others is the heart of any manager's job. R S F A

10. Positive encouragement and feedback are more effective at sustaining and improving performance than negative or confrontational feedback. R S F A

11. Openly admitting personal short-comings, vulnerability with others enhances trust and builds shared commitments. R S F A

12. I welcome and seize every opportunity to teach others what I know and what I have experienced. R S F A

13. The ideas, thoughts, feelings, and opinions of the person being coached are as valuable as those of the coach. R S F A

14. I am a continuous learner and work consistently on my own self-improvement. R S F A

Once you have received the feedback from others (see next section), complete the Intentional Coach Analysis of Results on page 38.

INTENTIONAL COACH—OTHER'S ASSESSMENT*

Circle the response to the following statements that reflects your experience with this person. Be completely candid and honest.

Response Choices

(R) Rarely   This person rarely feels or thinks this way. In fact, most of the time the opposite is true.

(S) Sometimes   Infrequently, this person may believe and/or act in this way, depending on the situation and the other person.

(F) Frequently   This represents this person's honest beliefs in most situations with most people; there are however, times and situations when he/she doesn't act/feel this way.

(A) Almost always   This is deeply rooted in this person's belief and value system and influences his/her thoughts and actions directly and consistently.

This Person Believes That	Rating
1. People in the workplace have unlimited capabilities; learning, growth, and change are always possible.	R S F A
2. Job position or title does not ensure one person to have power or authority over others.	R S F A
3. Healthy, positive, trusting relationships directly contribute to producing better business results.	R S F A

*Developed with the Learning Design Group.

4. Collaboration produces better results than   R S F A
    individual efforts.

5. People in the workplace want to improve,   R S F A
    make contributions.

6. Mistakes or errors can be opportunities   R S F A
    for learning, not just punishment.

7. The coach can learn as much as the   R S F A
    person being coached.

8. People need frequent, honest, consistent   R S F A
    feedback on what's going well and what
    needs to be improved.

9. Effective, frequent coaching of others is   R S F A
    the heart of any manager's job.

10. Positive encouragement and feedback   R S F A
    are more effective at sustaining and
    improving performance than negative
    or confrontational feedback.

11. Openly admitting personal short-   R S F A
    comings, vulnerability with others
    enhances trust and builds shared
    responsibility.

12. Teaching others what he/she knows or   R S F A
    has experienced is a valuable use of
    his/her time.

13. The ideas, thoughts, feelings, and   R S F A
    opinions of the person being coached
    are as valuable as those of the coach.

14. Personal improvement and   R S F A
    development need to be pursued
    consistently and continuously.

1. Which two or three beliefs from the above list represent this person's **strengths**?

    _____

2. Which two or three beliefs from the above list represent this person's **areas for improvement**?

    _____

Intentional Coach Analysis of Results

Use the cumulative data and respond to the following questions:

1. Which components of "intentionality" are your strengths (i.e., those that were rated overall "F" or "A" and/or those selected most often by others as your strengths)?

    _____

    _____

2. Which components of intentionality do you need to build into your belief system (i.e., those that were rated overall "R" or "S" and/or those selected most often by others as areas for improvement)? What makes this hard for you?

    _____

    _____

3. What beliefs, past experiences, or habits do you need to change or overcome in order to increase your coaching intentionality?

    _____

    _____

4. What are the benefits to you and those you coach if you are successful?

    _____

5. What are the consequences to you and those you coach if you are not successful? _____

_____

SELF-INVENTORY #3

Now as you consider your own insights from this chapter, take a moment and complete the following questions as a coach, weighing your responses in the context of the transition to being a coach.

1. What implications are there for you as a coach as you assess your own transition? _____

_____

2. Where you are today in coaching and where you would like to be?

_____

3. What areas of transition are the most important of all?

_____

_____

4. What areas of coaching might you choose to pay special attention to inside the coaching relationships you are currently engaged in? _____

_____

5. Which skills as a coach do you most admire in coaching and which qualities of a coach would you like to nurture in yourself? _____

_____

6. Who will support you in this process and be *your* coach?

_____

_____

7. After you have completed the intentionality self assessment, what activities or practices might you create for yourself that would further enhance your skills, qualities, and beliefs as a coach? _____

_____

Now that you have gained additional insight and perspective on your world as a coach, let me offer one final perception that a coach, James Flaherty founder of California-based New Ventures West, a coaching company, shared with me. He said, "As human beings, we often desire to live in a different, improved world. But we often end up enacting the very world we currently live in, thus creating the comfort zone we have come to believe is best for us."

In working with managers all over the world I have found that part of growing and developing means living with and working through change. It also means letting go of past behaviors, beliefs, and practices that no longer serve us well. You now are better positioned at the intersection of being a coach versus only acting like one. Which path will you choose to take?

3

So Now You're a Coach

Doing Things Right, and Doing the Right Things

One enlightening discovery in my work with business professionals was their efforts at being a coach took on the struggle of answering simple questions like: "What do I really do all day long as a coach?" "How would this change affect my work environment and life?" Time after time, session after session, I discovered that line and staff managers could talk about it, describe the role, and romance the notion of coaching, but they had real difficulty with *being* a coach in their real worlds of work.

What is the payback for you to be a coach, when it does appear that firms desire managers to be coaches but don't support the change fully? What's the point when job descriptions, positions content summaries, the proverbial internal rating and point system do not reward managers with salary increases or perks for *being* a coach? Most firms focus on the bottom line.

"Sure, we want you to be a coach, but you'd better make budget, hit your targets, make your numbers, and meet the plan" describes the usual messages.

The real message from companies is often that coaching is something the manager or employee does after hours or at the end of the day. It is my belief that coaching is not an either-or proposition. Instead, it is the prevailing spirit by which the manager or employee, or coach, approaches doing one's job and relating with people, as an hour-to-hour, day-to-day experience. It is really the "how-to" of the communication process. The payback is job fulfillment for everyone involved.

Coaching is the blend and planning of the right content with the appropriate delivery to ensure a more successful acceptance of the message by the receiver. Coaching in business is good business. However, not everybody does it very well. Often, people who are trying to be a coach do not know how to pull it off. Frankly, they end up doing much more harm in their efforts than if they had done nothing at all. Why? Well, because nobody likes surprises, except for those who enjoy people jumping out of the dark shouting "Surprise!" at a birthday party. Too often, the wanna-be business manager does not make the shift from manager to coach. Generally they are unclear about what a day looks like at the office, plant, or facility as a coach. Is your picture blurry too? It takes more than a quick swipe with a little corporate cleaner and elbow grease.

In the quick-fix approach to training and corporate initiatives that we discussed earlier, coaching becomes the flavor of the month, and adequate time for the stabilization and training of a new culture is not given. Companies offer a corporate seminar on coaching and then expect managers to go back to their old work environment that has not changed and renegotiate a new role with team members who now are expected to see the manager in a new light. They have had no training in this new culture. This is like sending amateur weekend auto mechanics into Mr. Goodwrench's shop and telling them to start working on the new models, because cars are making a funny noise in the engine. As silly as it sounds, there are many managers, coworkers, team members, and others wandering around their company, attempting to function as a coach. They are not given the tools and do not have the foggiest notion of how to do it. Compounding the problem is a system or environment that prohibits asking for and receiving help to be a coach. Asking many managers to let go of telling people what to do and to stop directing every move coworkers make—after they have perfected these behaviors for years—is a big deal.

Changing the corporate culture is an ongoing learning experience. Another crucial insight, as mentioned in Chapter 1, is that in sports the coach eventually picks his own team. This choice rarely occurs in the business culture. Sure, over time the business coach may have this opportunity. The luxury of hand-picking the team in business is reserved for the highest levels in the organization, while typical front-line managers must deal with what they have. This is a very sobering thought. You as the business coach will realize that in all practicality you must make the most out of the talent you have.

> I remember working for a maverick vice president of sales of a $3-billion food company who got so fed up with his managers hiding and protecting their better people that he wanted to propose holding a draft like in the National Football League, whereby the organization might benefit from moving and sharing the high-potential, highly-rated performers. This would allow the company as a whole, not the local manager or regional manager, to get the benefit of these top employees. Needless to say, this was viewed as a crazy idea and did not get much support from field managers. Why? Suddenly they saw their world becoming more complex and demanding.

This was unfortunate, because there was value in taking the risk to do something new, and the philosophy behind the idea was sound. It could have built in a teaching component by supporting the company as a whole to succeed.

Being a teacher is an interesting skill often cited by workers as a key competency for coaches. Letting people find their way and discover, rather than being told, is a key skill of facilitation by good coaches. I have learned as a coach that it may be quicker to just tell a person what to do, but then the solutions are limited to my perspectives and are based on only my experiences. When I share responsibility a team is formed, and infinite ideas, solutions, and outcomes are possible. Many managers fall short in critique/corrective action steps by focusing on what went wrong and by communicating, "Don't screw up; it's not okay to make a mistake around my shop." Too many would-be coaches have not learned how to operate in and facilitate win-win relationships. Their approach is best characterized as "my way or the highway," or my favorite, "I am flexible as long as you don't ask for any changes and you do it my way!" The changing landscape of work is shifting from control and a position of power to one of influence, facilitation, and support.

Coaching is becoming a core competency that makes sense for anyone interested in thriving in this new world of work. So, how do you feel about being a coach?

Perhaps you have wondered, "What are people doing when they are performing at their best?" That is a fundamentally different question than "What are the limits by which I can run my department and meet budget?" As a business manager, both of these questions are important to the success of the department or functional unit, or in business overall. But, they require two different mind-sets, skills, knowledge bases, and attitudes regarding how a manager goes about answering them.

Today's work environment is in upheaval, and times are changing. What was once certain is now more uncertain. At one time the model for managing was plan, lead, organize, and control. These words have undergone "cosmetic-business surgery" and have been replaced with descriptors like empower, influence, facilitate, stewardship, and coach. All too often, though, today's manager continues to act as if the future was yesterday. This is not entirely the manager's fault. Compensation plans, rewards, incentives, management practices, and organizational structures force many managers to operate under the illusion of contemporary approaches to managing. You may be inspired to change your style, but how does the top management see the light for supporting a company culture shift?

Don't get me wrong; I like managers. I am one! I direct the

day-to-day operations of Customer Inc. as a manager. However, a larger percentage of my time is invested wearing my coach's hat. Developing the managerial competence of coaching will enable managers of today to add sustainable competitive advantages for tomorrow, but only if they learn to be a coach and do it well and gain the support of company top executives fostering a new business culture.

In today's marketplace it seems like a monumental request to complete all the work that must get done within normal working hours. We are living and working in compressed times. The pressure to perform has never been more demanding and rigorous.

Some time ago I had the opportunity to attend one of those giant positive attitude/motivational rallies. You know the kind—where 14,000 people fill a sports arena, looking for the magic solution for success! The speaker I was most interested in hearing was Colin Powell. I was not disappointed. For me, he made two important comments that really fit the mood of the audience and the theme of peak performance. The first was: "Find in life what you love to do and really pour your heart and soul into it!" The second was when General Powell added: "In life, it's not what happens to you, but how you handle what happens to you that will be the true measure of your success."

Unfortunately, the vast number of workers, including those in executive positions, find themselves not pouring their hearts and souls into what they do, nor do they love their work. Too often, it's more like, "It's a living and it beats other stuff."

The sad truth is that a majority of people move through life and work with little pleasure or real feeling of significant contribution. Sure, by luck or circumstance they will have "moments of peak performance" as stated by author Charles Garfield. Far too many of these occurrences are brief, unexpected, unpredictable, and unrepeatable, and fade quickly into the past. However, some managers function quite nicely on automatic pilot as a regular approach to their flight plan of life. These people have often mentally checked out and are in maintenance mode throughout the day.

A very different reference point is used when thinking about and describing the role of coaching in business. The most successful role models as coaches are rarely cast in the image of being on autopilot. They are usually described as vibrant, enthusiastic, positive, forward-looking, upbeat, and lifelong learners. Are you ready for the challenge of becoming a conscious manager/coach, alive and vibrant? In no way do I want to suggest that traditional managers might not be described in similar fashion; they could be. The fact is, I have rarely encountered the same kind of passion and reverence for managers that I have seen for coaches in business.

What is it, then, that begins to differentiate the coach from the manager? Surely there are managers who function competently as coaches. More often than not, though, they are the ones who were cited by subordinates, peers, and bosses as the type of manager who contributed significantly to the development of others. They were ready to listen and learn from coworkers. I guess this quality of manager would be called a "natural coach." Some of you who are reading this book may find it an affirmation of your innate knowledge of coaching. Others of you have noticed managers with these coaching abilities and have wanted to gain and understand these skills. By reading and doing the Application Exercises in each chapter you will attain these skills. Over and over it was reported that these managers as coaches produced results on a more consistent level, with less hassle and turmoil, than those who operated out of a command-and-control style. By reading this book you will gain the knowledge to join these ranks. What helps a manager make a shift from one style of managing to another? Making a fine-tuned adjustment in your approach to working with others, moving closer to the coaching mentality, can make all the difference.

What causes the need for change? Can you remember reflecting back on a year and thinking about all the New Year's resolutions you made? Somewhere you conceived a vision of how you wanted to be, look, or act in some desired future state. When you saw this vision, you had already started to change. Changes can be spawned out of desperation (e.g., "I must lose 25 pounds") or made because "they felt right." New promises of change are not kept until there exists a deep sense of commitment, ownership, and *alignment between head and heart*.

This bonding of the heartfelt pledge and intellectual acknowledgement is what fuels outstanding individual accomplishment, success, and achievement. Change is not sustainable, repeatable, or replicable and will remain elusive if the ingredient of winning is only momentary. This is why what Colin Powell spoke about is so powerful and yet unpredictable and magical—when head and heart are aligned. When these ingredients come together in a coach, we call it charisma, charm, leadership, presence, and authentic caring. This coach is noticed because he or she possesses and fosters these rare and valuable qualities. The ironic thing is that you do have the capacity to create that which you truly desire to be. If *being* a coach is part of that step, let's create it together.

William James, the American psychologist and philosopher, has been credited with saying that "We only use 10% of our human potential." The coach recognizes the possibilities in others that individuals cannot always see for themselves. Why is this true? We often limit ourselves by our prior experiences. These mental screens provide a subconscious filter that affects our thinking and behavior. As humans, we all have a high capacity for excellence but sometimes we limit our output. We allow the possible to become the impossible! Another way to say this is that we don't always get what we want, but we do get what we expect.

Craig was a promising manager. He graduated from a prestigious university and went on to get an MBA from one of the top business schools in the country. After several successful assignments with his company, Craig was designated as a company fast-tracker or high-potential manager. This status qualified Craig to attend corporate training and the company's leadership development program.

However, a little negative voice inside Craig, also known as self-talk, played old undermining tapes in the his mind. Still, in spite of these messages he had a track record in business that was admired and applauded in the highest levels in the firm.

Then one day Craig was given a new assignment that stretched him beyond his capacity. It put him in a position he had not yet been in during his rise to fame. It would be his longest assignment, 24 months, almost double any other assignment. He would also encounter a series of poor former management decisions that had severely stunted the revenue of the business and had caused discontent. For the first time he was going to be in a hostile and uncertain position where there was very low morale. In short, as was reported to me by Jim, a battle-tested peer of Craig's, "The cakewalk is over; now we will find out what the guy is really made of."

This was all new terrain for Craig. The playing field had suddenly changed and he began doubting his own competence; his negative self-talk was winning. He began micromanaging—overcontrolling and making every decision—because of his fear of failure. The side effects of Craig's reactive behaviors manifested themselves in the management team becoming paralyzed. Everybody found themselves walking on eggshells. No one could make a move without Craig's approval. Unfortunately, Craig's demise came with pain to the organization and to those involved.

Craig's derailing managerial behaviors and thinking might have been headed off if he had had a coach who could see the blind spots he couldn't see for himself. Of course, Craig would have needed to be in a state of mental readiness to seek out a coach, listen to and accept the instruction, and then apply the practice prescribed by the coach. The coach would have revealed the fears and guided Craig's direction and style.

Craig's prior training and experience as manager had served him well in former situations; but situations change, become more complex, unusual, confounding at times. Managing in and of itself will not always solve the problem. You, perhaps, are familiar with occasions when the old adage "practice makes perfect" changes to "practice can make you tired," particularly if you are practicing the wrong things! There is a big difference between purely managing—which is about perfecting processes and systems to ensure that things run and work right—and coaching. Coaching is much more concerned with the identification of the right practices in changing environments and then practicing them in order to produce desired outcomes.

Deepak Chopra, author of *Ageless Body, Timeless Mind*, said: "If you are habitually frozen in past thinking, behaviors, responses, you will be unable to respond to the future."

I believe great coaches help "unlock the future" *with* the persons they are coaching. You will notice I didn't say the coaches unlock the future *for* the persons they are coaching. The goal of coaching is not to create a dependent relationship with the person being coached. Rather, the outcome of coaching in business is to create an environment where the learner becomes self-aware and self-correcting; thus, they become independent. We all have reason for being, a purpose in life, and coaches have an ability to help the employee, peer, and even boss see it more clearly.

To put a spin on the U.S. Army saying, coaches help those they are coaching "be all they can be."

I had an experience with an entire division of over 250 managers from a $500-million after-tax-profit business. The group convened in Arizona to chart the course of the next year's business strategy, and I was coach to the planning team as they tried to create a theme for the meeting that would capture the hearts, minds, and spirit of these managers, facilitating them to perform at the next level. The planning was slow and tedious, full of personal agendas, hidden emotions, and petty issues of power, control, and envy over who would get the recognition for putting together the meeting.

After many unproductive sessions and a breakdown in creativity, we achieved breakthrough. A manager who assumed a coaching role helped the planning task force focus on the game plan and released the binding that held the group in a deadlock. The coaching freed the group to shift into their best thinking, and each member made contributions to create a theme for meeting that would fulfill the lofty expectations of the division president. Appropriately, the theme of the meeting ended up being: "Getting people beyond the box."

What is the "box" corporate America is operating in today? It contains downsizing, right-sizing, reengineering, consolidation, divestiture, and layoffs. Workers in all shapes, sizes, and salary classes have become stressed, depressed, and fearful about their futures with work. The emphasis on creating shareholder wealth and beating last quarter's numbers is a predominant focus. What's the rebound? As reported by *USA Today*, 48% of workers stated that employees are committing illegal or unethical acts at work. The pressure on the workplace is explosive. Sure, one could take consolation in the fact that 52% of workers are solid corporate citizens. But, what are the deeper, ripple effects of managing a workforce where the data says pressure at work causes workers to act illegally or unethically?

The new way to run a company where the role of management is different is highlighted in the book, *The Customer Is CEO*, by Forler Massnick. He goes so far as to suggest that "it is impossible to truly have satisfied customers if you don't have satisfied employees," or internal customers. This happens in his view when an organization is focused on being customer-centered, and includes the mind-set that everybody has and is an internal customer. So one must treat employees accordingly.

The *USA Today* story on workers ended with the sobering feedback by workers saying that, "to help curb negative behaviors, managers should be better communicators." There needs to be much more open dialogue at work about what is going on. The vision for the company and management must make visible, serious commitment to management practices that enable workers to feel involved in the process. In the world of customer satisfaction, 80% of dissatisfaction has nothing to do with products; rather, the problem from the customer's viewpoint, Massnick says, "is in areas of service, relationship and interpersonal contact."

Where do firms invest most of their resources? Are companies investing in what the customer is concerned about? Too often, the investment is 80% in products and only 20% in relationships and employee satisfaction. If we expanded that thinking to the typical role of today's manager and the average day in the life of that manager, what might it look like? Research from the experts in time management indicate that 80% of the resources, time, energy, and attention that the managers invest tends to be in things like meetings, organizational issues, logistics, planning, budgeting, forecasting, and fire fighting. Are these important?

Of course these activities are important and sometimes they do encompass employee and customer satisfaction, but more often than not these "focus points" have nothing to do with what really matters, the care and feeding of one's team or human resources. Think about the possibilities of managers and the relationships they could have with people if they could alter and adjust the two ratios. Instead of managing things 80% of the time and attending to people 20% of the time, what if they would strive for more balance, spending 70% of the time coaching and 30% on managing the details. What would happen if a company's allocation of resources invested 75% into cultivating relationships and developing people and 25% into things, products, equipment, and technology? This move from the traditional approach of managing to developing the managerial competence of coaching makes good business sense. Why? Because over time not only will it produce better results, but healthier business relationships will also reduce hassles.

Emitt was the sales manager for an information services consulting firm. His main responsibilities included the sales and service of technology-related information systems to *Fortune* 100 companies in his region.

Emitt had sales, sales support, and service reporting to him. At that time he was more of a reactionary—a manager rather than a coach. He typically would spend 90% of his time chasing down people, dealing with service, and addressing hassles for the customers in the region.

Emitt was so busy doing things that he lost sight of what his real role and value to both his team and his customers was. He received his coaching from his boss and long-term mentor about the difference between *being* a coach and managing the region.

With some adjustments, including his own attitude about being a coach, delegating more authority to others, communicating clearly and regularly, and establishing boundaries around performance expectations, Emitt was better able to manage his time and set priorities for the care and feeding of his team. In the end everybody felt better, was more clear about what was expected, and knew who was accountable for what results.

This shift in Emitt's behavior and attitude allowed him to shift from just managing things and putting out fires to being a coach.

What are the differences between managing and coaching? Consider the following input from hundreds of managers, workers, and professionals from coaching workshops about the distinctions of managing versus coaching behaviors. The three lists to follow offer insights into the distinctions, often subtle yet obvious, between managing and coaching. I share these not in a manner to pass judgment but rather for your consideration as you interpret for yourself the differences between managing and being a coach. Incidentally, it is also true there are numerous and multiple approaches to both acquire and deploy these items in your portfolio of managerial competence.

COMMON MANAGERIAL PRACTICES

The first list contains activities that are distinct to managers. These would be distinctions common to just about all managerial assignments across corporate America in some variation.

- Preparing annual budget for business.
- Recruiting, hiring, and staffing for department.
- Writing department annual report.
- Running the quality initiative for business unit.
- Attending the corporate training seminar on diversity.
- Making a presentation to the controllers group.

- Searching for new ways to better serve the department's customers.

- Gaining buy-in to purchase new software from the division controller.

- Serving on the human resources task force on a new performance management plan.

- Creating work process flow diagrams for key process improvement.

- As prescribed in supervisor's manual, conducting annual performance reviews.

- Investigating employee complaint involving a form of harassment.

- Realigning roles and responsibilities of functions in work unit.

- Planning department off-site meeting to launch new strategy.

MANAGERS TRANSITIONING INTO COACHING

The second set of distinctions contains behaviors that become more blurred between managing and coaching. Clearly there are legitimate expectations on the part of workers that their managers should operate by and behave in ways that align with this list. The items in this second list would also be a part of coaches' persona.

- Communicating in an open, fair, and honest manner.
- Giving timely, clear feedback to others.
- Setting and communicating performance standards.
- Treating people with respect, trust, and dignity.
- Holding others accountable for their actions.
- Following up, being responsive, and acting on issues as promised.

- Remaining open, being able to both give and receive feedback.

- Respecting diversity, accepting others.

- Being positive, yet realistic about expectations.

- Walking the talk, aligning the behavior to the spoken word.

- Sharing the vision of the future.

- Being honest about the possibility of attaining the desired goals one is working toward.

- Being able to share both the good and the bad news with others.

DISTINCTIONS OF INSIDE-OUT COACHING

The third set of distinctions represents those attributes, competencies, and attitudes reported to me as embodying the essence of coaching.

- Giving guidance and options about the work being performed, without being overcontrolling.

- Giving both the technical knowledge for the job as well as the support to maintain a positive attitude to perform the job.

- Giving feedback in a manner that does not stifle the innovation and creativity of the individual being coached.

- Giving praise consistently for those actions that deserve positive recognition and the appropriate consequences for those actions that warrant corrective action.

- Giving open and honest feedback, free from political or personal-gain motives on the part of the coach.

- Giving help for overcoming barriers and obstacles that may prohibit the successful achievement of the goal.

- Giving coaching to help an individual think of options and alternatives for the problem and come up with possibilities that would not exist without the input of the coach.

- Enhancing performance by helping others evaluate themselves objectively.

- Openly discussing positive actions and/or opportunities where an action plan is mutually put in place to enhance performance, behavior, or thinking.

After reviewing these three lists you can discover the differences, preferences, and distinctions in managing and coaching. The business world of course needs both to forward success in the new cultures of business. Some managers are natural coaches, but the vast majority of managers miss critical opportunities to coach. By reviewing these lists you might add your own interpretations and notice where you fit in the mix. You will clearly identify with some more than others, offering you some new insights about yourself. Which ones would you like to acquire new skills in?

Warren Bennis, the management consultant, author, University of Southern California professor, and speaker, was first to describe leaders in terms of "doing the right things" and managers as "doing things right." These concepts are both right and vital to the success of the enterprise, but an obsession with only "doing things right" potentially sets the manager up as having a finely tuned department with all the appropriate process, controls, plans, and systems in place but, in essence, zombies for workers. Why? What may be missing is the human component as in our discussion of coaching as a core competency for managers, supervisors, and senior leaders of the organization. Some firms have even expanded this concept; their performance management process includes the idea of peer coaching and 360-degree feedback as a tool for the development of high performance.

From a coach's perspective, it's not so much where you start; it's where you end up that determines the winners and achievers in business and in life in general. A very interesting case study from a manager's perspective may help point out both the subtle and the obvious differences between coaching and managing.

> My assignment was to assist a division management team with the implementation of the company performance management process. Part of the training was skill practice in effective communication. I vividly recall one triad (three managers) working on the following case study:
>
> "As a manager for the company and responsible for several departments, you have initiated an effort to enhance teamwork not only in your own area of responsibility but also companywide. In the past, the firm has been very close-knit and had fostered a sense of family. You know that for the most part, that feeling of family has eroded badly and given way to solos, each doing their own thing. *In actuality, the company had been operating more like a confederacy than a union.* Now more than ever, lines of authority have transformed into picket lines used in skirmishes along the flanks of departments and functional units. For uncertain reasons, not really known to all, you and other peers have not made public this initiative, and even so you have sensed pockets of resistance, ambivalence, and apathy, as well as hostility at the prospect of moving the overall effort forward." What would you do now? Why?
>
> As I moved around the room, which, by the way, represented a cross section of both functions and levels of employees, the group that was struggling the most was a group of three managers. They were in the middle of gridlock! It appeared clear to me, but not to them, that their thinking and frame of reference on how to approach solving this dilemma were very much centered around perceived losses of control, status, work, power, information, stability, rules, and procedures. They were even concerned that they would be perceived as weak because their staff currently looked to them for the answers.

Now, by no means do I want to imply that all managers represent this type of dogmatic, rigid, and structured approach to interpersonal conflict and managing differences. I have studied this notion of changing the essence of managers to coaches, or at least strengthening the coaching competency in managers. The shift must be heartfelt first, then embodied deep inside the manager. The manager needs to be both willing and able to transition to this new way of being.

I feel very fortunate to have had the opportunity to meet and work with world-class authors, thinkers, and speakers. One of the very best is Robert Kriegel, author of many books, my favorite being *If It Ain't Broke . . . Break It!* In the book he says, "The only people who really welcome change are babies with wet diapers and busy cashiers. No matter how positive the change, most people try to avoid or resist it." He goes on to add, "Change is disturbing. The natural tendency is to stick with what we know, play it safe, gravitate toward the familiar."

There is the famous marketing story of how Xerox Corporation's failure to anticipate, respond quickly to, and adapt to its changing customer needs allowed new entrants like Canon into the market and eroded Xerox's long-standing leadership position in copying. Another example occurred in the rivalry between Notre Dame and the University of Southern California when the USC Trojans were playing host to the Irish of Notre Dame. As the first half came to an end, Notre Dame held what appeared to be a commanding lead. But USC and its coaching staff made adjustments, while perhaps the Irish believed they had the game won. In the end, USC won the game by a score of 55–24!

Thanks to the innovation of television today, veterans in the world of sports, particularly former coaches, have found life after coaching to be as rich and fulfilling as when they were active as coaches. One of the most recognized and knowledgeable is John Madden. His expertise and perspective on the upcoming game feature some rendition of "keys to victory," or, in nonjock talk, what is it that must go right for each team, in order for the team to win. Now, odd as it may seem to non–football fans or non–sports enthusiasts, this discipline of gazing into the competitive sports future actually has its roots in business strategic planning under the heading of "critical success factors."

In almost every high-level business strategy session, there is also some rendition of critical success factors and the impact they may have on the execution of the plan. I introduce this final element into our discussion as a truly critical component of the coach's game plan.

In 1980, a group of young Americans, mostly college students, stunned the world by winning the gold medal in ice hockey at the Olympic Games. They beat teams that, at least on paper, were better than they were. The Europeans had dominated the world competition for years, specifically the Russians. But this team of overachievers was different.

The approach by their coach was different as well. He told them, they were "a team of destiny."

Further, Herb Brooks, the coach, did what many coaches fail to do: First, he clearly defined the "keys to victory," the critical success factors for this team to win and defeat the world competition. Next, he created a set of practices (*doing things right*)—the right activities, the schedule, the process, the controls, and measurements to assure success. Then he combined the element that separates coaching from purely managing. Brooks made sure all of his planning happened *at the right time* to ensure winning.

Herb Brooks had mastered *doing the right things*. He was brilliant and let Craig Patrick do what he was good at, manage things. This freed Brooks up to excel at what he was world-class at, coaching, and get the team to play at a level higher than what they dreamed possible. He was also able to create team cohesion and, as my colleague Chris Majer, founder of Sportsmind, says, "manage the mood" of the team.

Now, as you go back and consider what you have just read in this chapter, I invite you to continue on with the Application Exercise and stabilize your new learning.

Application Exercises

SELF-INVENTORY #4

Learning to be a coach is not easy. There are those who believe that coaching is a simple task; don't let them fool you. Coaching requires a distinct set of skills, knowledge, and attributes. One of the first steps is awareness, so be honest in your Self-Inventory. Ask yourself these questions, and perform the activities. Write and record your responses in your journal and reflect on them.

- In thinking about those you coach, what is it that people are doing when they are performing at their best?

- Think about the many activities and tasks that you are engaged in daily.

- Make two lists, one a "doing the right things" list of activities that are truly coaching in nature, and a separate list that is "doing things right" in nature—management, supervisory activities that are part of your job but are not coaching and so on, (e.g., procedures, tasks, etc.)

- In reviewing your second list, which items might you consider letting go of in an effort to focus on "doing the right things," or, in our discussions, doing more coaching and less managing?

- When you reflect on your own personal comfort zone, could you consider expanding your own thinking to go beyond the "box"? Are you free enough to see and discover different possibilities for yourself as a coach (e.g., investing more time in the care and feeding of people and less on tasks that you could delegate or not do at all)?

- Make a list of what restricts you.

- As a manager in business, what have been your critical success factors?

- As a coach in business, what success factors are you seeing that you could include in you new work culture as a
  coach?

- Are you ready to increase your competencies as a coach
  and further strengthen relationships you have with those
  you may be coaching?

You are increasing your coaching effectiveness just by your
willingness to do this inventory. You have already started to
let go of your control and are learning to step outside of your
personal comfort zone—your box—and develop yourself and
others. Growth will come each time you do an Application
Exercise. Congratulations! You are becoming a coach, because
you are becoming coachable.

The following excerpt from *Call Me by My True Names* by
Thich Nhat Hanh might be helpful as you think about your
transition to being a coach and increasing your coaching effectiveness.

> The boat people said that every time their small boats were
> caught in a storm, their life was in great danger. They also said
> that if it happens that there is one person on the boat who keeps
> calm and does not panic, that would be a great help because the
> personality of such a person would inspire faith and confidence.
> People would listen to him, keep serene and there is a chance for
> the whole boat to come out of danger.
>
> I have said before that our Earth is somehow like a small boat.
> Yes, compared to the other beings in the cosmos, it is a very small
> boat and it is in danger of sinking. We need such a person to in-
> spire us with calm confidence, to tell us what to do. And who is
> that person? If you are yourself, if you are your best, then you are
> that person. And it is only with such a person, calm, lucid,
> aware, solid, that our situation could be avoided.

4

Convenience, Speed, and Doing More with Less
The Myth of the 'Quick Fix' Coach

In a society turned upside down, sideways, and any which way by change, it can be tempting as a coach to adopt a quick fix approach to coaching. With reorganization, downsizing, and right-sizing, the pressure and challenges to survive make the quick fix look inviting. Whether it is short-changing training or sacrificing the long term for instant wins, there are consequences for the choices the coach makes. This chapter will enable you, the reader, to better understand the seduction of the quick fix.

It seems as though every day we face the temptation and seduction of solving life's problems with short-term expedients. At times, if you are like me, it's easy to say sure, why not? Why take the extra step when you don't have to? As our world becomes more complex and smaller through advances in technology and communication, it's also easier to have access to data, information, and knowledge without the rigors of really learning the materials.

One example of the instant solution formula:

My 12-year-old twins were given the assignment of writing a paper for their sixth-grade geography class on Latin America. Prior to our family buying a computer, that learning process would have included a trip to the library to research the appropriate books and reference materials to write the report. Now, the process is done in half the time, over the Internet, with the on-line encyclopedia. In an instant there are printed pages on the subject.

This instant fix gives an immediate feeling of "I am done." Now, perhaps you are saying, "So what's the big deal? Aren't there benefits to using the computer for learning in school?" The obvious answer is yes. The downside—and my point—is what gets lost in the fast-track process. The easy access, the lack of rigor and discipline may leave out the ability to understand and know the material, as opposed to getting the information. The bigger issue is the long-term expectation young people develop for other parts of their lives.

Another example of the thirst for the instant solution comes out of the world of selling and sales training. In the old days, the image of the traditional salesperson was that of the shyster, the huckster, the hustler seeking to quickly romance and manipulate the unsuspecting buyer into a quick sale. The method of training salespeople was to teach the 15 or 20 tactical power closes. In other words, you learned key phrases, with emphasis on the emotional and psychological hot buttons that would touch people's inclination to buy something.

However, the customer today knows more. That kind of razzle-dazzle, smoke-and-mirrors mentality of selling gave way to a more consultative approach. The salesperson both thinks and behaves like a consultant. The focus has become seeking first to truly understand the customer's needs and then attempting to find the best total or complete solution for the customer.

I recall working with a company on the development of coaching for their district sales managers.

The project included a discussion of the quick fix mentality in coaching. The first day ended with lively debate over the pressing issues of not enough time to coach, difficulty in defining what coaching is, and the behavior of jumping in to save the sale. Instead of teaching salespeople how to sell, district sales managers were trained to tell the salesperson what to do. The sales managers were not given the tool of asking questions or skill of "inquiry."

All too often the sales manager falls into the trap of telling the salesperson "what to do" and fails to develop critical thinking skills in the sales rep. These dilemmas helped to frame the search for authentic coaching competencies and instruction for the managers as they functioned as a coach. Thus, not using the quick fix became a more developmental approach to training.

How do you create this shift in thinking, reducing the enticement of the quick fix?

This shift from managing to coaching is a mental shift made prior to the acquisition of any skill. This step makes a huge difference in your success as a business coach. Too often, managers automatically assume that they are coaches and/or that coaching is not all that difficult—anybody can do it! As mentioned earlier, this is the outside-in approach and traditionally manifests itself in words sounding like coaching, but actions that are from the old hierarchy system. Although there are some natural-born coaches, being willing to let go of the quick fix and your success as a coach will grow as you continue to seek true mastery.

Finding a compelling method to imprint in the minds of these managers that the quick fix method would not develop coaching competence is a challenge. What do you need to know in order to truly learn about *being* a coach? There are new and different sets of skills, knowledge, beliefs, and attitudes that you need to take hold of in order for you to make the transition.

As I was preparing for a workshop and munching on the hotel's rise-and-shine early-morning breakfast, this illustration came to me:

There in the business section of the morning paper was a cluster of advertisements. There were at least four different organizations all creatively saying, "Lose weight fast and easily! Acquire the look and image of a healthy, trim, well-toned body without the trouble and hassle normally related to weight loss." There were three other ads of a similar nature. They all formed a visual and I saw how to use these attention getters as a means to illustrate the seduction of the quick fix.

I opened the day's meeting with operations managers about the romance of the quick fix in operations management. I used the example of the quick fix in weight loss. They immediately got the point that nothing worthwhile, of lasting value, comes without a certain amount of legitimate effort and work. As an operations manager, wanting to apply coaching to the daily efforts of improving the results of operations is both an admirable goal and one that requires a unique set of skills.

The weight loss ads provided me with a concrete example of how we are living in times of instant gratification for our wants and desires. It is all around us, in the arts, health, business, education, travel, and technology. We can acquire that which we seek in very short time frames. However, what is the cost of this?

There are hidden costs in a quick fix mentality. Two of these are the learning that does not happen during the development of new skills, and the loss of appreciation for how much time, creativity, effort, or talent is required to complete certain work or accomplish a goal. My belief is that the rush to attain that which we desire to possess blurs the learning and practice required to become competent at what we are attempting to learn.

By no means am I saying we should not have access to acquire that which we seek. But, by heightening your awareness to the quick fix *cost*, you can weigh which is the more creative path for you to gain new insights and learning.

To wage the process of coaching from the inside out takes time. In wine making, the process cannot be rushed without damaging the wine. So it is when it comes to learning how to be an effective coach.

Sure, one can accelerate the learning process with intense

and rigorous practices, but there are still basic principles of adult learning that must be adhered to. One usually doesn't wake up one morning with a sudden inscription on the subconscious mind, "Learn to be a coach!" There must be a certain readiness, mood, and heartfelt need to learn that inspires someone to be a coach.

New learning and contexts for learning must be integrated with what is already in existence. The adult learner must see the clear fit between the new stuff and his or her prior stuff (knowledge and past experience). This is one reason why so much corporate training doesn't stick on the job; the process of connecting the past, present, and new learning is left out.

Once the adult learner has been exposed to new concepts and thinking possibilities, he or she must have a set of clear practices to map out the regular development of the new skills and behaviors. In the world of formal education and organized sports, the principles of research assignments, projects, and practice are keys to the learning process and true change from the inside out. That's why the Application Exercises are key to your success.

Coaching is checking in and getting feedback as your learning progresses. These important elements make the difference between excellence and outside-in coaching. For some reason, in the world of business this is often a missing element in working relationships. It seems that the whole phenomenon of work, with all its components, lacks the regular ongoing quality of communication that is present in other forms of relationships. Many managers in business miss the connection here about the role of coaching.

Once the coach has communicated progress, then there must be some form of consequence for the achievement of learning—some application, results, or lack of them! This step is usually avoided because of fear. An example comes out of sports medicine and conditioning:

The Olympic gold medal U.S. hockey team in 1980 enjoyed their success due at least in part to their tremendous physical and mental

conditioning. The training was led by coach Jack Blatherwick, a PhD in math. Not only did Jack apply mathematical equations and statistical correlations to training, but he also drastically transformed the way world-class hockey players, coaches, and trainers approach the conditioning of Olympic and professional athletes. His book, *Overspeed—Skill Training for Hockey*, creates a road map for youth, college, and Olympic hopefuls to follow to dramatically improve their ability to perform at higher sustainable levels.

At the end of the book, he challenges coaches to consider the model of Japanese business, as well as Russian athletes' training philosophy and practices in creating world-class players.

He writes of the then Soviets, "When they first started playing hockey, they were not interested in the 'quick fix' approach, nor were they interested in the occasional miracle win. They wanted their national teams to dominate consistently so they prepared their youth."

I have heard business leaders address their organization in similar terms. I also found Blatherwick's creative approach to the application of the sciences to sports fascinating. The message, even after it was proven by the U.S. hockey team (Olympic gold medal, 1980), is not always accepted, because of the allure of quick fix gratification and short-term win mentality.

Studying best practices in nonrelated fields leads to breakthroughs in applications within any chosen field.

I worked with a health care clinic to help the clinic staff, including physicians, think of their patients as customers. This was "out of the box" thinking because of the long traditions and practices of the medical profession.

What is learned? Customer service departments, just like the clinic's staff, must heal things after they are sick. Sure, you can argue—and rightfully so—that there is a big difference between repair of sick patients and relationships, but the underlying principles are the same. The clinic staff's ability to respond accurately and quickly under adverse conditions is the reflex action that only comes with practice and over time, working together serving its customers (patients). Once the health provider saw the fit between patient satisfaction as being equivalent to customer satisfaction, the new learning could take hold.

Shifting to the driving force behind the team is the business coach. The bottom line is that in the development of coaches and of coaching competencies ongoing attention, care, and feeling are required. It's worth repeating: Coaching requires the development of a unique set of skills, attitudes, and competencies acquired *over time*.

Perhaps you are known as someone who approaches life from the perspective, "I have life pretty well figured out, so don't tell me otherwise." Then you tend to be a person who leaves little or no "wiggle room" for contribution or learning. Your outlook on life may tend to be black and white, with few gray areas. Do you sometimes like to finish a sentence for others and answer questions before they are asked? Do you like to let people know what you know? If these are true or partially true of you, your first challenge will be to learn to be more coachable. It's time to shift your thinking to include others and make the space for "wiggle room."

Let's be clear here: You are not bad and are not doing it wrong; you are often talented, gifted, and an on-your-feet thinker. You have and will continue to succeed in your life, but with any success there is a price to be paid. The issue here is a mind-set change from being nonnegotiable to being open and having a degree of willingness to tolerate some ambiguity in your life. This is about continuous learning and improvement.

I am going to suggest that a more successful position to operate from is the mind-set of *thinking like a beginner*. You will always develop ways of being curious about the unknown—and, by the way, this option of thinking creates more possibilities as well. Instead of approaching problems in life with the past heavily driving current thinking (closing off possible notions because they won't work), use an approach where you can operate as what the Reverend Robert Schuller would call a "possibility thinker."

Look at Figure 4-1. It is simply one interpretation of the "think like a beginner" mind-set. Being willing to be more flexible and negotiable with others is critical to your success. Each of our minds has a realm of "I know that." Over time, we learn to

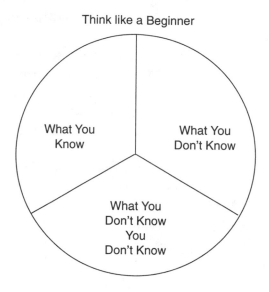

Figure 4-1 *Think like a beginner chart.*

get dressed, eat, drive a car, balance a checkbook, and so on. In short, we know thousands of big and little tasks that require little or no new thinking. This is excellent, for we wouldn't want to have to learn every day how to make toast!

There is another realm of our mind that we might refer to as "I don't know that." Here are things that we either don't know about or, after we learn about them, we then reflect back and say something like, "Gee, I guess I didn't realize that!" If you are like me, sometimes this is common sense.

The last realm of our mind offers the most significant opportunity for breakthrough learning. Its defenses are also the most difficult to overcome and the scariest for most of us to confront. It is the realm of "I don't know what I don't know." For many of us, our ego lives in this realm. Of course, our ego is very fragile, and can be easily damaged. Some of us approach life and risk taking with an invisible Handle with Care sign on our chest, or "you can't get through my armor." Because of this resistance to experimenting outside the known world, many live comfortably in their comfort zone. This, of course, is okay, but beware of the possible limitations this kind of mind-set begins construct-ing around you.

Often, the quick fix approach is a welcome remedy to staying in the comfort of the known zone. By and large, the seduction of the do it now, get it quick, fast temporary relief is born out of the inability to sustain the exploration into either of the other realms. At times we venture into the "I don't know that" realm, but very definitely not into the realm of "I don't know what I don't know." This is where a competent coach can make such a monumental impact and difference for those he or she is coach-ing. Much of our effort in life is tied up in the search for what-ever we are currently working on or pursuing at the time. *We tend to find comfortable behavior to quickly get us to our desired goals and outcomes.*

The movement from the known to the unknown can be very scary. It seldom comes easily and is a monumental task without a map of where you are going. A coach can not only help pro-vide the map, but also provide direction and support in helping you reach your desired changes, unlocking what you don't know that you don't know. This process of change and transfor-mation doesn't stick to the tried-and-true, the comfortable, and the world you know. Your thinking changes to risking in the world you don't know, but the process can be made smoother with practice.

Practice, when consistent, planned, and repeated, helps to re-define old skills and create self-confidence in new ones. This is where many would-be coaches in business fail to help those they are coaching make the successful acquisition of new skills, attitudes, and behaviors. Instead, they resort to the quick fix, simply telling the person what to do and having them do it.

Yet, when I think about this new work environment in terms of where future coaches come from and how coaches are promoted to head coach, it's an interesting study. For ex-ample, in the world of sports, the lesson has been painfully learned that just because a former athlete excelled as a player, and perhaps even achieved greatness as a player, he or she may not automatically succeed as a coach. Why? Because the very skills, attributes, and intuitive moves of a great player are significantly different from those required to be a successful and great coach.

There have been very few success stories in sports of the fabled player-coach. The point here is that in business, the lesson has not been learned or applied well. Success as a player does not automatically mean success as a coach. Success as a technician (functional competence) does not ensure success as a manager, and then a coach. Many managers are great players, but can they transition to *being* great coaches? How about you?

In business, all too often the super salesperson is promoted to sales manager; the high achiever is fast-tracked through the organization, serving short-term assignments and being labeled as having high potential. One outcome of this is that in business the coach may be unaware of the need for designing practice. Here is an example:

> Lee Harris was a tremendous salesperson. His closing percentage is still the highest in his company! No doubt Lee had "the touch." Lee was promoted to sales manager because he could sell, not because he could manage or coach.
>
> There is a famous scene in the movie *Glengarry Glen Ross* where Alec Baldwin plays a sales manager and announces the new sales contest to the sales associates—played by an all-star cast, including Jack Lemmon. The sales manager says, "The rules are . . . first place, a new Cadillac El Dorado; second place, steak knives; third place, you're fired! Oh, by the way, if you get the steak knives, you might want to use them on yourself."

Sure, this is Hollywood, but similar realities are out there on the street! Often, business managers, acting as if they are coaches, ask, prod, or even demand changes in behavior, performance, and thinking from their employees. In fact, Lee Harris operated like that at times, and, like the Baldwin character, used the old style of managing and control to get results. These directives and/or commands, often cleverly disguised as coaching, are vague and offer no guidelines or game plan as to how to go about taking the necessary steps to make changes in behavior, attitude, and action.

In contrast to this scenario, think about the process of teaching someone something that you know how to do well—perhaps your hobby or recreation. You know the subject matter well, and you are competent, knowledgeable, and skilled at this activity.

Now, assume for a moment that you are going to teach this to others.

What are the steps you might go through? What would you need to know? What precisely are the outcomes you and the others are looking for? Why are they so interested in learning how to do what you know how to do? What experience and level of past knowledge (if any) do they bring to this learning? What kind of learners are they? Do they bore easily? Are they passive or proactive? Do they like personal stories? What process will you use to teach them? What materials do you need? How much time do you believe it will take? How will you communicate and measure success? What do they expect from you? What do you expect from them? These and other questions are what you need to answer in order to think like a coach.

The coach must consider multiple options prior to the coaching process by choosing the practices that will best fit the learner. Yet, in business this is often not the case. The would-be coach expects the learner, almost through mental telepathy, to see what is to be done. This idea, the quick fix, as opposed to the planned and insightful design of specific practice, is what grabs attention and focus. Getting it done quick, fast, to save time to do other things rules the day and behavior. And then there is disappointment when the desired results are not there.

I reflect back on my conversation with Lee Harris.

Lee was failing in his role as a coach with Jan Crown, a sales rep in his region. We were speaking about his relationship with Jan, who was responsible for two large and significant accounts.

Lee said, "Jan is talented and bright, and really does a nice job on precall planning. She also has a great sense of the market and

the competitive position we have with accounts and competitors."

"So, what's the problem, Lee?" I asked.

"Well, I think she overtalks on sales calls."

"Hmm. What evidence do you have of this?"

Lee got suspicious. "What are you asking, Jim? I just know she
talks way too much and the customer seems not to get a word in
at all! You know, Jim, from my early days of training, I learned
that salespeople should not do all the talking. They should mostly
listen."

I asked, "Have you shared this with Jan?"

"Sure I have. I've told her on numerous occasions to back off,
don't talk so much, and come up for air! I told her to ask more questions, to play back what she hears the customer telling her. Take
care of any customer concerns, then handle their resistance to buy,
and finally, close the sale!"

"Sounds reasonable to me, Lee, but I notice you are giving Jan a
whole lot of your thinking. Have you ever asked her for hers?"

Well, yeah, kind of, but she doesn't get it."

I asked, "Last week you went on a market visit with Jan; on that
trip, what did you do about this dilemma?"

"First, right away I told her she must ask more questions. Second, I had to jump in a couple of times on different calls to save the
sale, and man, am I glad I did!"

"Oh?" I said.

"Yeah. I think Jan really knows how important it is to ask questions now and to keep the conversation going to close the deal. I
think the coaching session was a pretty good one. She did finally
agree that I was right and that asking questions will help her close
more deals."

"So, what's your sense about her willingness and ability to apply
your coaching, Lee?"

"Good question. Truthfully, I am not sure," Lee responded with a
dazed expression.

In subsequent conversations I had with Lee about Jan, he continued to be frustrated. As a matter of fact, their relationship de-
cayed further over time. I can't help but compare and contrast

Lee's style of coaching and what I have asked of you while considering teaching somebody else.

Do you see a difference? How would you have coached Jan?

As a coach you can be tempted to take quick fix approaches to solving problems. Most of the time these solutions provide only temporary relief at best. This chapter outlined the need for a more lasting and solid approach for improving performance and for producing enhancing and satisfying relationships between coach and the person coached. Do you see the potential in your work situation?

As it has been our practice at the conclusion of each chapter, apply yourself to the exercises. You have the opportunity to design for yourself practice(s) that will enable you to better transfer your key learnings from the reading into your real world. Like the coach training a world-class athlete, the business coach includes several fundamental components in the conditioning process.

QUESTIONS AND ACTIONS—DESIGNING THE GAME PLAN

This practice session will assist you in planning for when you want to coach, as well as coach you in designing specific practices for the person you are coaching. These are not quick fix tactics and will require you to think about what you want out of coaching, as well as ask you to consider what the person you are coaching expects out of the learning. Start the practice session by contemplating the following questions and doing the activities.

1. What kind of coaching session is this and when do I coach?

2. How intense is this coaching?

3. Plot out where you see this coaching initiative being with regard to the levels of competence chart on page 76, and consider the kinds of skills and quality of relationship needed depending on where you are on the graph.

4. What are the competencies of the individual you are coaching? Assess the level of competence of this person.

5. How will your coaching vary depending on the desired outcomes and the competence of the person?

6. What are the gaps between current performance and desired outcomes?

7. Consider the level of trust you have with this person; is it high or low?

8. How will this level of trust affect your coaching?

9. Think deeply about the romance and allure of the quick fix to coaching and contrast those thoughts with your answers to the questions just completed.

PREPARING YOURSELF

When am I needed as a coach when?

- When things are going well and I can recognize, reinforce, and reward positive behavior.

- When I would like to suggest small, subtle mid-course adjustments.

- When things are not going well and clear corrections need to be made.

- When breakdowns, significant behavior and attitude problems, skills gaps, or performance issues exist and must be addressed.

HOW WILL I COACH?

There is no best style of coaching. In fact, many different styles can be successful in a variety of settings. Your challenge as a coach is to consider your options, choose the one(s) most appropriate to the coaching situation, and then remain open and flexible to coaching conditions.

COACHING INTENSITY

1. Again using the levels of competence chart below as a guide, plan your coaching.

2. What skills are needed based on the type of situation? How are they different (if at all)?

3. What type of coaching situation is most difficult (challenging) for you as a coach, and why?

LEVEL OF COMPETENCE

Beginner	Novice	Intermediate	Advanced or Master
Little or no skill, knowledge.	Some skills, knowledge.	Applied skills, knowledge.	Accomplished skills, knowledge.

1. What differentiates the levels of competence? (Write out your own definitions of each type of competence shown in a person.)

2. How would your coaching change by level of competence?

CLARITY OF PURPOSE

Reflect on these questions and write the responses in your Application Exercises section of your journal.

1. What is it you as the coach are trying to enhance with this person (i.e., attitudes, knowledge, skills, or behavior)?

2. What performance standards have you established? How have you communicated them? What are the mea-

surements and consequences of performance or lack of performance?

3. What is the practice construct? What does it consist of? What are its framework and timing?

4. How will you structure your communication loop? How do you plan on giving feedback? Can there be more than one source of feedback? How do you ensure readiness on the part of the person being coached?

5. Who will coach the coach? In other words, where do you as a coach go to seek support, fresh ideas, and objectivity regarding your assessments and practice assignments if you so desire?

Now you may feel a bit overwhelmed, but sturdy, solid mental scaffolding is needed to support you while constructing yourself as a coach; don't be alarmed or feel you are alone. All coaches at every level of competition—must go through some parallel course of thinking if he or she is to truly improve the members of the team!

It is the coach who sees the possible holes in the player's game. The combination of the coach's knowledge of the business, the coachee's willingness to learn, and a structured methodology for practice, with appropriate feedback and support, improves knowledge, skill, and attitude. When this occurs, the process can be replicated as needed.

CLARITY OF THE SITUATION

1. Think of an upcoming coaching situation.

2. Whom will you be coaching?

3. What outcomes do you wish to achieve?

4. What is the current level of this person's performance?

5. Where are the gaps? What is missing today in the performance of this individual?

6. What one area are you going to focus on in your coaching with this person, and why?

7. How will you structure your practice for the improvement of performance with this person?

8. What measurements, rewards, and communication process will you use in your coaching?

9. How will you communicate progress with this person?

Congratulations! You have taken a significant step in the creation of authentic coaching practice for yourself in business. You are moving beyond the quick fix to lasting value. In the English language we have two uses for the word "practice." As you have discovered, it can be a verb, meaning taking an action, or a noun, a thing. As a coach, you can design those specific practices that help enable the person you are coaching improve his or her performance, and at the same time you as the coach are creating for yourself a true coaching practice in business. Where do you think you are in the process? Where do you want to be? Are you willing to make the appropriate moves to enhance yourself as a coach? What will those moves look like for you?

5

Turbulence

Coaching through Ups and Downs, and Staying the Course

Five o'clock on a bitterly cold January morning in Minnesota.

The light at the side entrance of my house shone like a beacon in the dark as the cab approached along the deserted street, plowing through snowdrifts and careening across glazed ice. In just the time it took to load my bags in the trunk, my hands were frozen stiff, and my head ached from the minus-40-degree windchill factor. But I wasn't complaining. I'd be outta here soon enough.

A little later I was on Flight #1228 to Palm Beach.

Newspaper in hand, hot coffee and Danish on the tray in front of me, I thanked my lucky stars I was headed away from the Land of 10,000 Frozen Lakes. In a few hours I'd be poolside, soaking up the Florida sun and thinking back on the Minnesota winter with the guilty pleasure of a kid who'd gotten away with raiding the cookie jar.

I drifted off, only to be awakened by the voice of the pilot.

"Well, folks, this is the captain. As you can see, I've gone ahead and turned on the Fasten Seat Belts sign. Air traffic control is advising us of a little weather in the area, and we'll be encountering some turbulence for the next twenty minutes or so. Sorry for the inconvenience, and we'll do everything we can to make the ride a little smoother. So, sit back and relax—and thanks for riding with us today!"

Now, I don't know about you, but when I hear "turbulence" at 33,000 feet I feel about as relaxed as I would in the front car of a roller coaster. My heart pounds, my stomach churns, and my eyes race wildly about the cabin looking for the exits. I stare blankly at the newspaper, seeing not the story in front of me but the next day's imaginary banner headline featuring the fatal crash of the plane I'm on.

On top of the world one minute and a basket case the next. Never mind that the ride seldom turns out to be as rough as I'd anticipated. Or that I've never even had a close call. When I hear "turbulence" my mind and body go on autopilot.

As a result, if I'm traveling on business I can't concentrate on my work; if it's a pleasure trip I can't enjoy myself. But there is a silver lining: My reaction to turbulence in the air has taught me something about the way we handle other forms of turbulence—in our lives, in business, and specifically in coaching.

For turbulence surrounds us. As we go through life, we inevitably encounter updrafts and downdrafts—disturbances that upset our sense of equilibrium and security. We can't avoid them. But we can gain the skill to steer through them, maintaining our balance and staying on course.

I've come to believe that it's not turbulence that causes us trouble. It's our reaction to it. On the airplane, it's not the choppiness of the ride that upsets me—it's the commotion inside me. By the same token in other stressful situations in life, our emotional and biological responses often wreak more havoc than the original problem.

Dr. Robert Eliot, famous cardiologist and former member of NASA's medical team, talks about the price we pay for inappropriate responses to stress in his book *Is It Worth Dying For*? Toward the end of the book, Dr. Eliot offers this basic rule for living in a stressful world:

Don't sweat the small stuff. And the corollary is it's all small stuff!

I carry my own version of this thought with me on an index card in my pocket as a daily reminder of our power to redirect our responses to turbulence.

You can't fight and you can't flee. But you can learn to flow.

Chances are at some time or another you've had to deal with someone whose idea of coping with turbulence is to beat it down at the source (the source usually being some unfortunate person!). Dr. Eliot describes these people as "hot reactors." You could also call them big spenders, because they put out big bucks' worth of energy on pocket-change-sized problems. Take Keith, for example.

A senior executive in a major multinational corporation, Keith always knew exactly how to respond to any threatening, disturbing, or unusual situation: He went ballistic. Sometimes he did it for no apparent reason at all—other than to keep his staff on edge. They were on edge, all right. "Who knows what he'll do when he hears about such-and-such," managers would mutter nervously as they headed into meetings with him.

Keith knew he was a bully. And I think he justified his bullying to himself on the grounds that it produced discipline in the ranks. But what he didn't know was that at a deeper level he didn't choose to do it at all. It was a reflex. When he encountered stressful situations he went on autopilot. In his case, that meant protecting himself by intimidating others.

As a result, his division was going nowhere. A hunkered-down, make-no-mistakes attitude prevailed, squelching innovation and creativity. In fact, placating Keith had become the division's chief occupation, to the detriment of the business.

To my great relief, Flight #1228 landed uneventfully in Palm Beach. As I pulled my baggage from the overhead compartment, I thought about how it was not only the pilot but also numerous team members and resources I had to thank for my safe return to terra firma. To begin with, there were the training, people, and equipment that prepared the pilot to fly. Then there were air traffic control, sophisticated radar and instrumentation, flight books detailing airport layouts, the flight crew—all in place to get me from Minnesota to Florida without so much as a drop of spilled coffee on my tie.

Yet as we navigate our own lives we must function in all the roles. And that's a tough assignment. Our internal radar doesn't always detect approaching disturbances, and we're caught by surprise. Turbulence jolts us off course; we struggle to regain control. Suddenly the flight plan is worthless. You are on your own. What do you do?

Just as Keith's autopilot kicked into flight mode when turbulence threatened, Anne had a flight reaction.

> Anne, who managed the payroll department at a large company, valued her relationships with staff members and avoided conflict at all costs. Her idea of coaching was noninterference. And she got by with it until turbulence came along in the form of a major departmental restructuring. Two of the supervisors who reported to her actively resisted the changes and began feuding with each other over turf and responsibilities.
>
> Not wanting to alienate either of them, Anne stayed out of the conflict, hoping things would eventually settle down. They didn't. The situation deteriorated. The change process was stormy, one of the supervisors quit, and the department was left scarred and torn by the experience.

If you compare Anne's reluctance to take control to a pilot who expects the plane to fly itself through a storm, you immediately see the problem. But the other extreme is just as bad.

> Chris brought impeccable credentials to his new job as general manager of a large manufacturing firm—an MBA from one of the most prestigious business schools in the country, a successful mil-

itary career, and a winning track record managing several different businesses. Not surprisingly, considering his military background, his management style was based on command and control. He gave his troops their marching orders and called it coaching.

But, his new assignment involved building a team from a highly diverse group of managers, from different companies and cultures, with widely varying belief systems and views. It quickly became apparent that something wasn't working. The troops weren't falling in line! With their level of talent and experience it should have been a crack outfit. Instead, the harder Chris tried to push, prod, and command success from the team, the more they dug in their heels. In short order, he had a thoroughly demoralized, unproductive unit on his hands.

Out of sheer frustration, Chris agreed to get some coaching, and came to recognize that his autopilot behaviors were getting him in trouble. Trained as a commander, he had never caught on to the concept of teamwork. In his conviction that his own ideas were best and determination to make sure they were executed properly, he had never considered the possibility that team members had anything to contribute. As a result, the team felt undervalued and resentful, Chris felt isolated and unappreciated, and the business suffered.

The moral? You can't coach effectively, especially when confronted by turbulence, unless you can override your emotional autopilot and switch to your inner equivalent of manual controls. Only then do you have the flexibility to respond by learning from others and adjusting to the conditions around you, rather than reacting reflexively.

Not that this is easy. As Earnie Larsen says in his book, *Who's Driving Your Bus?*, "For years [people] have practiced becoming who they are. Learning begins at an early age."

It takes time to unlearn the old ways and internalize new ones. The encouraging news for all of us, according to Earnie Larsen, is that "some behaviors fade out naturally, and appropriately, as we outgrow them."

For example, you probably don't fight with your brother over who gets the bigger slice of pie anymore. On the other hand, faced with conflict and stress, patterns of behavior we thought we'd laid to rest a long time ago spring back to life, flawlessly preserved—as anyone can attest to who's suffered through family gatherings where mature adults revert to childhood roles and conflicts.

Actually, some of the most valuable lessons I've learned as a business coach have come from my sons—all five of them. As the father of two sets of twins plus one more boy for good measure, I've been, shall we say, very well motivated to understand how to influence kids' behavior.

What I've discovered is that in order to make a difference in my sons' behavior, I need to develop different practices for myself. Here's a typical scenario:

> I'm scrambling around the house in the morning, trying to get myself ready for work and get the kids ready for school. Utter chaos. I'm pulling my socks on with one hand, tugging on my tie with the other—and getting all steamed up arguing with the boys about what they are going to wear: "That doesn't match. Those pants have a hole, that shirt is dirty. Now *this* looks good. What do you mean, you don't like it? Mom and I spend a fortune on clothes for you guys and I can't pay you to wear them!"
>
> This went on every day until finally, at my wit's end, it dawned on me that we really didn't have to go through all that. A minor disagreement had been blown up into a monumental battle of wills, and it wasn't worth the fight. I decided to let the kids choose from two or three outfits the night before, so we'd be all set the next morning. It worked like a charm.

So why hadn't I stumbled on this simple solution sooner? I was so caught up in the turbulence of the power struggle between us, it didn't occur to me that I was causing more trouble than the boys were. When I finally allowed the smoke to clear, I saw that my own behavior didn't work and that if I changed for the better, the kids would too.

Whether you're dealing with four-year-olds or 40-year-olds, being able to choose your own actions is your most powerful tool in shaping the performance of others.

I have learned to force myself to slow down, look, listen, and think before deciding how to act in a stressful situation. If I can step back, observe my own behavior, and then choose the most effective coaching response, I can work with turbulence rather than being worked over by it.

In other words, the more alert you are to your autopilot behaviors, the more readily you can override your counterproductive responses and switch to behavior that you choose. The greater your mastery of your own responses, the greater your ability to understand and influence the performance of the people you coach. By learning to recognize your autopilot behaviors, you as the coach can help others to unlock their potential.

Coaching is a state of mind—and not one you can arrive at overnight. It's a journey, a process of continuous improvement requiring new practices to move you to a new way of *being.*

Hey, wait a minute, you may be thinking. *This sounds suspiciously like therapy!*

True enough. I do, in fact, sometimes suggest therapy as a tool for building coaching effectiveness! But even if you're put off by the idea of therapy, it's important to realize that your competency for coaching others grows out of your capacity to know and develop yourself. So the question is, who coaches *you?* Coaching can come from unexpected places—if you're open and ready to learn.

Which brings to mind the story of a boy called John, who played on my oldest son's hockey team his senior year of high school.

John was a kid who'd never had it easy—not at home, in school, or on the ice. But he had a lot of heart and kept plugging away. Year after year he struggled to improve his game, never quitting, always hustling. Even though the coach thought of him as only a spot player, playing him only if someone got hurt or hit a slump, he kept on going.

The story opens at the beginning of a season when, for the first time in umpteen years, players, parents, and fans felt the team had a chance at the state hockey tournament. However, the team got off to a dismal start. With the team loaded with talent but saddled with a 1–4 record, people began questioning the competency of the coach.

Then the team held a development session led by Chris Majer, president of Sportsmind, an organization focused on helping teams achieve superior performance. As Chris watched the team practice, he observed that they seemed out of balance—in his words, "off-center." After a discussion about the mental part of individual and team performance, Chris led the players through a series of "centering" exercises designed to build confidence, inner strength, and power. For several of these exercises he happened to work with John in a demonstration role.

The very next game, John, who had never been a great goal scorer, scored in the first 30 seconds of the first period! The following week the team took a road trip to northern Minnesota, the mecca of the state hockey scene, and John kept it up, scoring goals in each of the first two games and going on to become all-tournament. While the team struggled to win only one game in three, John was on fire!

I'm convinced this story would have had a different ending if only the coach had been as open to growth and change as John. But rather than learning from what Chris had accomplished, and changing some of his own practices accordingly, the coach seemed threatened by John's leap in competence. Instead of encouraging John and building on his progress, the coach began ignoring him, failing to praise his accomplishments. Finally he benched the kid. It was as though he had to prove to himself that he hadn't been wrong about John's potential.

The spark went out. The team finished the season losing far more games that they won and the coach resigned the following year. John graduated from high school, joined the Army, and as far as I know, never laced up his hockey skates again.

It was a tough season for everybody. But I came away from it with a new appreciation of how powerfully turbulence can affect a coach. If you asked the coach whether he wanted John to play well and the team to win, he'd say, "Of course! What a crazy question!" Yet, the coach's reaction to the turbulence he felt over Chris's success with the players was so counterproductive that he actually sabotaged the gains John and the team had made.

Turbulence can take the form and shape of a wide spectrum of events, circumstances, situations, and settings—from high school hockey in Minnesota to girls' tennis in California, a critical client presentation, or a new process at the plant. The point is, how do you respond as a coach to the inevitable onslaughts of turbulence?

John's story parallels an experience I had as a business coach.

When I met her, Rosemary was struggling with a thorny assignment. She had been promoted to head of her department in a major publishing company, over several of her more experienced colleagues. One day, she was their peer; the next, she was their boss.

For one person in particular, Will, this was a bitter pill to swallow. For years Will had been the right hand of the former department head, handling a wide range of administrative tasks. He thought, reasonably enough, that he was being groomed to lead the department, and felt betrayed when it didn't turn out that way.

His extreme resentment spread throughout the department, creating an atmosphere in which it was difficult for Rosemary to accomplish anything. Backstabbing was the predominant mode of communication, and every initiative she undertook seemed to be sabotaged. The department's problems weren't lost on the company's leadership, and if they had a more shortsighted perspective, Rosemary might have been out of a job. Instead, recognizing her potential for leadership despite her struggles, the company arranged to have her work with me to develop her coaching skills.

As we talked, it came up that she had never actually confronted Will about his behavior. We agreed that this moment of truth was long overdue. As Pat Riley points out in his book, *The Winner Within,*

The coach makes a covenant with the players, in which they agree to live by the "core values and beliefs" of the team. Right up front, there has to be the understanding between coach and players of either being with me or against me.

Rosemary needed to have the kind of open, direct conversation that all coaches must have in order to be successful. In a coaching session with Rosemary, I invited her to consider how the turbulence she and the department were experiencing was tied to Will's behavior. While it's not the most enjoyable aspect of coaching, confronting conflicts and nonconformance is a vital skill.

Rosemary decided that her success in communicating her concerns to Will would hinge on her ability to set aside her own feelings of anger and resentment toward him in order to deal with the observable behavior changes she expected from him. She realized that the longer she remained angry and defensive in her own thinking, the less capable she was of accurately interpreting Will's intent.

By lowering that defensive posture in communicating with Will, while being laser-clear about expectations, boundaries, and consequences for nonconformance, Rosemary was able to work with him collaboratively in improving their relationship and ultimately the performance of the department.

Here is the game plan Rosemary developed. It can give you key insights as to how you can develop statements that change automatic responses to turbulence while coaching others.

- I will use "I" statements in speaking.
- I will speak in the here and now, rather than in terms of some unclear time.
- I will acknowledge and be responsible for my own feelings and judgments, and guard against introducing them into the conversation in an attacking manner.

- I will recognize the difference between feelings, behaviors, and desired outcomes.

- I will clearly communicate desired goals, outcomes, and standards of performance instead of merely reacting when someone is not meeting my expectations.

- I will be genuinely interested in what is said, and listen intently in order to understand the coachee's position.

- I will neither attack nor avoid, but actively listen, first playing back feelings, thinking, and behaviors of the other person when dealing with conflicts.

- I will demonstrate my clear understanding by reflecting back issues.

If John's coach had gone through a similar process, the outcome for everyone and for the individual team may well have been different. The coach could have more effectively tapped into John's unique abilities, thus allowing for more contribution.

We do not control the events that surround and influence our lives. If we simply react to them, our options are limited. If, on the other hand, we can make ourselves more flexible, probing, and open to change, we can create a different set of possibilities for ourselves, resulting in genuine self-confidence and increased personal effectiveness. As Stephen Covey says, "Win the internal victory first, and then turn outward to effectively coach others."

Past experience, beliefs, expectations, and interpretations of the world are some of the key factors that make up our flight plan on autopilot. Automatic response, positive or negative, can dramatically alter our coaching effectiveness.

If we first recognize that we all have a built-in response system and that we can learn to better direct it through increased awareness, we are ahead of the game. Skill building and practice lead us to producing different options and possibilities for our behaviors in stressful situations.

You can always choose your response. Once you are aware they are automatic, this is very powerful. These insights can give you hope, courage, confidence, and the knowledge that no matter what situation you are presented with as a coach you can influence directly your component of the coaching relationship. Your attitudes, behaviors, and great coaching practices give you new approaches to winning life's challenges. You have it within you to develop a range of alternative choices to respond more appropriately to coaching opportunities.

As you work through the next set of exercises, think about how turbulence affects your coaching style, and what you can do to stay on course, whatever ups and downs you encounter.

Application Exercises

Think about the inner conversations you go through in the various ups and downs of your life. Reflect on those situations that cause you to burn energy on turbulent situations.

DETECTING TURBULENCE

Name five of the biggest sources of turbulence in your life.

1.

2.

3.

4.

5.

CHECKING YOUR AUTOPILOT

What are the emotions and thoughts you automatically experience in reaction to the turbulent situations you named in the preceding exercise?

1.

2.

3.

4.

5.

YOUR AUTOPILOT FLIGHT PATTERN

What nonproductive behaviors do you have in response to turbulence?

1.

2.

3.

4.

5.

CHOOSING MANUAL OVERRIDE

Thinking about the preceding exercise, what alternative behaviors could you choose for each that would be more effective and productive?

1.

2.

3.

4.

5.

How do you feel about dealing with those turbulent issues in your life now? Perhaps you've gained some new insights about coaching successfully when the going gets rough. Whatever your own thoughts are, keeping these basic ideas in mind will support you as you develop your coaching skills:

- You are in a unique position as coach! You can enhance the thinking, attitudes, beliefs, behaviors, and ultimate outcomes for those you're coaching.

- You have the ability to manage your own reactions and responses to turbulence.

- You can create a new set of behavioral choices for *yourself*, thus improving your ability to coach others through life's ups and downs.

- You are the CEO of the most important company in the world; it's called You, Inc, and you are in charge!

6

Chalking the Field

Drawing Up the Rules of the Game

From sandlot games on up, every organized sport has a defined playing field. *Ballpark, arena, court, pool, field, track, course*—the words bring to mind vivid images of matches, action, players, teams, and champions.

While these fields of play are as different as the Anchorage-to-Nome Iditarod Trail dogsled course is to Scotland's St. Andrews golf courses, they all serve the same basic function—to impose order on what would otherwise be chaos. Individual sports venues may have their quirks—the "Green Monster" at Fenway Park, the grass courts at Wimbledon, and Heartbreak Hill of the Boston Marathon, to name a few. But they all still conform to an agreed-upon set of standards. Boundaries are clearly marked. Likewise, the rules of the game are universally understood and accepted, so players show up knowing exactly what to expect and what is expected of them.

Unfortunately, the same can't be said for business. New employees, technologies, competitors, market conditions, organizational structures—they all create different and continually changing rules to work by.

That's why, unlike sporting events where players walk out onto a field with the boundaries already in place for all to see, in business the coach has to establish those boundaries with every player on the team. This process of delineating the rules and expectations for performance at work is what I call "chalking the field."

Without a chalked field, the business team will be in turmoil and ultimately lose—not because they are lousy players, but because they simply don't know what to do! *What's expected? How will we be measured? How do we know if we're winning or losing?*

Of course, in sports athletes know the rules of the game inside and out before they ever make the team. Great coaches make a point of establishing responsibilities, accountabilities, and expected results with each player—the process Pat Riley calls "creating a covenant."

But you don't have to look to the professional sports arena, the shop floor, or the boardroom to understand the power of this process. Getting expectations and communicating them clearly differentiates the business coach from an average manager.

When my neighbor Vera's husband died at the age of 40, she was determined to keep as much continuity as possible in her children's lives, which meant stretching herself to relate to them in ways she hadn't before. So when her daughter Lynn's soccer team needed a coach, she volunteered—even though she'd never done anything like it in her life.

It seemed like a great idea at the time. But, as the season approached she began having second thoughts. How would the team members and their parents react to her when they discovered that she didn't know what she was doing? She could have backed out at that point, but being someone who was always ready to learn new things and explore new territory, instead she geared up.

She went and met with several other coaches in the association to get their ideas and support. She checked out a pile of soccer books from the library, and immersed herself in the history, rules, and strategies of the sport. She even watched an ESPN special on legendary coaches.

Before the first practice, Vera hosted a pizza party for team members and their families. When everyone had had a chance to get acquainted and grab a slice, she stood up to speak.

"I'm new at this, and I'm going to need your help. Coaching this team means a lot to me. I can't tell you how many times I used to look out the window and see my husband kicking a soccer ball around the yard with a bunch of kids. They'd be out there for hours having the time of their lives. Well, I don't want to lose that.

"My goal is simple—for everyone to grow, have fun, and be the best they can be. I'm learning about coaching soccer. But I do know about working hard and learning together. I'm going to work hard to make this a great season for all of us. And I know by working together and working hard, we'll do big things as a team."

Vera went on to lay out her expectations about the players' responsibilities and the role parents could play, the commitment of the local soccer association, and so on. And when she was finished, she had won everyone over so completely, she had no trouble signing up experienced assistant coaches and a team manager. She even recruited a kid's German shepherd as team mascot!

What Vera accomplished right from the beginning was to arrive at an understanding with the team about where she was coming from, and how they could work with each other. The positive response she got from team members and parents suggests that the ability to communicate clearly and openly is sometimes just as important as experience in coaching.

This simple life experience opened my eyes to critical components of coaching in business. I have found in delivering business coaching workshops around the world that successful coaches are willing to be open, honest, vulnerable, and trusting with those they are coaching. They also recognize that even with considerable competence, experience, and expertise there will always be times when the appropriate solution or approach may not be apparent to them—but is perfectly clear to another member of the team. The important lesson for managers who aspire to be coaches is *learning to be open for change.*

World-class coaches don't get that way with an "I have life figured out" mentality. They are negotiable, flexible, versatile, and willing to look for win-win solutions. This isn't to say that successful coaches aren't direct, disciplined, straightforward, tough, take-charge leaders—they are! But they are also fair, concerned, supportive, and deeply committed to the ongoing development of those they are coaching. That's the difference between chalking the field and plain old butt kicking.

Whether the coach initiates a chalking the field discussion, or it is launched by an employee or peer seeking coaching, some essential elements need to underlie the conversation:

1. Building trust.
2. Cultivating a relationship.
3. Developing continuously—team members and self.
4. Being open to new ideas.

BUILDING TRUST

Trust is the cornerstone of the coaching relationship. Vera established a relationship of trust with her daughter's team through her own openness and honesty about her background, strengths, weaknesses, and goals. Key factors in coaches' ability to build trust include:

- *Reliability.* Live up to your commitments.

- *Consistency.* Say what you mean and mean what you say.

- *Acceptance.* Be accepting of others for who they are, reserving judgment and staying open to different approaches and styles of performance.

- *Competency.* Continuously improve and learn new skills.

- *Respect.* Be respectful of yourself and the people you coach.

CULTIVATING A RELATIONSHIP

Just as in tennis, swimming, or track, the real work in business coaching is done one-on-one, over time, in a relationship between coach and learner. Contrary to our popular images of coaches in action, it's not a matter of the occasional pep talk or in-your-face showdown when the going gets tough. For you to be a successful coach, be closely and continually involved with your players; observing, interacting, and responding to your team members' development needs is key.

DEVELOPING CONTINUOUSLY—TEAM MEMBERS AND SELF

Vera's aim as coach was to help everyone "be the best they can be" for herself and the team. Simple enough! We take it for granted that this is the goal of any coach in sports. But for some reason it gets more complicated in business, where all too often the coach's agenda is to control or even compete with team members.

As my friend Howard Dallin, who's an accomplished actor, playwright, and director, puts it:

> *When I'm directing, I'm not acting. I'm not memorizing lines, wearing the costume, or standing in the spotlight. I'm there to support the cast, to help them bring their performance to its highest level, not compete with the actors.*

I came across a fascinating program on the BRAVO Channel the other evening, called "Inside the Actors Studio," which featured an interview with Paul Newman. Asked how his background as an actor affected his approach as a director, Newman said that actually he worked with each actor differently, but that his goal was always to give actors the freedom and confidence to experiment and stretch their limits in shaping their roles.

Great coaches continually seek opportunities to learn and improve their own performance, as well as their players'.

BEING OPEN TO NEW IDEAS

In their book, *Built to Last,* Jim Collins and Jerry Porras describe successful companies as having the ability to preserve their core ideology while at the same time achieving growth. They go on to write about embracing the "genius of the and" and letting go of the "tyranny of the or" instead of operating from a position of either-or thinking.

Here, for instance, are some typical either-or statements in coaching situations:

- *My team can be either creative or conservative.*

- *Either we stick our necks out and jump on immediate market opportunities, or we play it safe and go for the sure thing.*

- *Our organization will either be tightly aligned or be free spirited and individualistic.*

If you recast those statements, keeping in mind that a mutually trusting coaching relationship allows many valid strategies for winning the game, they might go like this:

- *My team can be creative and also conservative when called for.*

- *We can take advantage of immediate market opportunities and use sound business judgment.*

- *Our organization is aligned in vision, and allows considerable latitude in achieving the vision.*

It's critical for the business coach to see the wisdom in the "and"—to see that life is seldom purely either-or when it comes to dealing with people. Let me make it clear, though, that what we're talking about here is ordinary coaching conversations and interactions about everyday workplace issues, not seriously deviant behavior or the violation of codes of conduct. Issues concerning integrity or core values are not negotiable.

In these coaching conversations there are two parts. Part one is the content of the message, and part two is the delivery of the message—in other words, what you say and how you say it. We'll talk about the "how you say it" piece at length in Chapter 7, which explores the language of coaching. But before we do, let's take a look at how several of the success factors we've already discussed come into play in a chalking the field conversation in a business situation.

When Martha, a regional sales manager at a large cosmetics company, walked into her quarterly market review session with Rita, vice president of sales, a full 25 minutes late, Rita could hardly conceal her irritation. *Now I'll be late for my meeting with the ad agency,* she fumed silently. *Besides, you'd think with sales this shaky the least Martha could do would be to show up for our appointment on time.*

"I apologize for being late," Martha began as she came in the door. "The traffic was unbelievable. Let me get the monthly report—"

"No need," snapped Rita, more sharply than she intended. "I've already seen it. My question is, what are we going to do about it?"

"Well, let's back up a moment," Martha said. "If you look at these notes. . . ." She fumbled with her briefcase, which suddenly popped open, dumping papers all over the floor of Rita's office. There lay the report—without the notes she'd clipped to the front. Her mind flashed back. *Damn! I must have left them on the kitchen table this morning,* she thought in a panic. *How could I have been caught so unprepared?*

What are your reactions to the first few minutes of the conversation between Rita and Martha?

Rita broke the silence. "Martha, we've got to put some spark back into your salespeople to make up for lost ground here in the third quarter. I don't think there's anything seriously wrong with your team, but what can we do to jazz them up a bit?"

Martha fought to regain her balance. "I know we've been struggling. But the numbers have improved slightly, and I'm encouraged by the orders that are coming in now." *There! Would that satisfy her?*

"Yes, and I've appreciated your e-mails on those developments. But I still have this gnawing feeling that we aren't where we need to be!"

What does the woman want, blood? Doesn't she know how overwhelmed we all are around here? Martha sputtered, "Remember, back at budget time we agreed that those targets were very ambitious, considering market conditions. Nothing has really changed to improve our position since then. In fact, our advertising and promotional support was reduced by twenty five percent, and that's killing us! Combined with the problems between the customer service group and my sales team, it's no wonder we're in the soup!"

If you were the coach in this situation, what would you do next?

Why doesn't she just take responsibility for the business? I don't want excuses, I want results. Just tell me how you're going to fix the problem, thought Rita. She glanced at her watch and sighed. "So, here we are kicking off the fourth quarter, Martha. How do we get back on track?"

There are always times when a coach must be direct, no-nonsense, and firm, with a tone that is not a personal attack.

At this point it's not only the sales situation that's derailed—it's the coaching conversation. Both people are spinning their wheels. Rita is battering away at the same point without making any headway, Martha is stuck in full defensive mode, and the chances of accomplishing anything positive at the session are virtually nil. What went wrong?

Distracted by peripheral issues (Martha's lateness and the resulting backlog in her jammed schedule), Rita wasn't able to communicate openly and effectively with Martha. Rita may have thought she was being honest and direct in her attempts to outline her expectations for Martha. But she was inwardly seething at Martha for messing up her day. And her not-so-hidden anger was causing Martha to read her frank comments as attacks—and give unproductive, defensive responses.

This could have been an opportunity for both business executives to switch to their "internal manual controls" and override their autopilot behaviors, so that they could navigate more successfully through turbulence.

If Rita had been cultivating an honest, open relationship with Martha all along, she probably wouldn't have gotten so angry about the delay, assuming that Martha was unavoidably held up. Without that residue of anger, she could have been much more receptive to Martha's ideas and point of view, and more effective in chalking the field. She could have moved away from either-or thinking, and sought an "and" solution instead.

"But wait" you may be saying. "Doesn't Martha share some of the responsibility here? Isn't this coaching business supposed to be a *mutual* relationship?" Yes, of course; that's why working toward mutual acceptance and expectations is so critical.

In short, coaching is a two-way street. Let's look at what a mutual relationship in a coaching session might look like. Notice how both the coach and the coachee respond to each other in this coaching relationship:

Sue, head of a food products company's customer service group, was meeting with her boss, Russell, to discuss the business plan she had developed. After some warm-up conversation about Sue's move to a new house, Russell said, "I've heard about the progress your team is making in putting this plan together. You've come up with some excellent ideas. Did you get the e-mail I sent you about it?"

Sue answered, "Yes, I shared that with the team. They really appreciated the recognition."

"Where do you see us going next, Sue?" asked Russell.

"Well. . . ." Sue hesitated a moment and thought to herself. *Things are going so well. Should I tell him about the delays in the order entry system?* She plunged ahead. "Actually, we've run into a major snag in the installation of the new order entry system, and that's going to mean some delays in implementing the plan."

"Oh?" replied Russell. "So where does that put us?"

"I'm taking full responsibility for it," said Sue, trying to sound confident and on top of things. "Not only for the system itself but for the overall smooth running of the department."

"I appreciate that," Russell responded. "Can you fill me in on what you're doing to get things back on track?"

Shoot! Sue groaned inwardly. *I should have known he wouldn't let it go at that.* She thought for a moment, then said, "We're in the throes of deciding what our next steps should be. I've put together a team to work on it, including my people as well as staff from accounting, information technology, sales, distribution, and operations. And the vendor for the system has also committed technical consulting. The team is going to select the best of two alternative approaches we've identified, and have a fully documented report on my desk a week from today."

Russell probed again. "And you're sure the team will come up with a long-term solution that we won't need to rework ninety days from now?"

"Russell, we both know nothing's sure, other than death and taxes. But I do feel good about the team and the way they're handling the job. And I'm confident they'll come up with an effective resolution to the problem."

Russell sat back and grinned. "I'm counting on you."

Sue returned the smile. "I won't let you down."

What do you notice about this example as compared to Rita and Martha's conversation?

In this exchange, there's real trust and mutual respect between coach and manager. Sue didn't have to tell Russell about the problem with the order entry system, but their relationship was strong enough that she felt she could. As a coach, Russell does more listening than talking. When he listens, he grasps not only the words spoken, but the emotion and intent behind those words. This enables him to get the information he needs without being overly interfering or controlling. He is open to Sue's approach to solving the problem, even though he may well have done it differently. This also reflects his ability to focus on the present and not be on autopilot, only reacting to Sue's work.

Their relationship enables them to agree on goals, rather than tactics. Sharing expectations or chalking the field together allows for win-win accomplishments. Accountabilities are clear, and appropriate measurements are in place to track results. Because they respect each other's competence, Russell does not micromanage. He doesn't invest time checking every move or decision Sue may make. The environment they work in is one of risk taking, rapid response to problems, empowering, and enabling due to clarity of communications and trust. As a result of this coaching, Sue is not just buying into an approach that her boss would prefer to have her take, but rather is choosing freely to solve the problem and own the outcome. It's the difference between mere compliance and true commitment to the job.

Compliance offers the illusion of commitment. Too often, the manager assumes the employee is fully behind the plan, only to be disappointed later when behavior does not follow the spoken word. Commitment, the act of being accountable for results, can transpire as the coach and person being coached mutually agree and freely choose to honor the promise to perform. The difference between compliance and commitment is that the individual finds a way to get it done no matter what, as opposed to giving up at the first sign of adversity. Can you see how and why it is important to mutually chalk the field with your associates?

This relationship took time to develop, with many chalking the field conversations shaping a coaching environment of trust and respect. Russell was able to tap the inner resource in Sue, which resides inside all of us, waiting to be unlocked and applied. Do you agree? Are you working in a similar situation? If so, what makes unlocking the unique inner resources inside us so special? If you are unable to tap into others' inner power, what might you try differently?

As we come to the Application Exercises, remember that you as a coach have the right and responsibility to clarify and communicate expectations, standards, and consequences for living up to the covenant you create with those you coach, or for those who don't.

The investment you make in planning, preparation, and conducting chalking the field conversations will produce dividends for you and those you coach. Relationships will be more productive, with less hassle and much higher levels of mutual trust and satisfaction for all those involved.

CHALKING THE FIELD IN YOUR COACHING CONVERSATIONS

Now it's your turn. Keeping in mind the critical success factors we discussed earlier in this chapter, use these exercises to chalk the field for your next coaching conversation. Ask yourself these questions:

1. What do you want to accomplish with this person?
2. What boundaries are you willing to set up and stick to?
3. Which areas are negotiable and which ones aren't?
4. What are the goals for this person?
5. What are some of the different ways he or she could get there?
6. What strengths, needs, concerns, and experience does the person bring to the relationship?
7. How can you outline your expectations without being overly controlling or prescriptive?
8. How might you open the conversation to frame your intent and establish a climate of trust, respect, and mutual gain?

COACHING—FACE-TO-FACE DISCUSSION

The objective of this Application Exercise is to review and share your ideas about coaching, as well as the ways in which you respond to coaching situations. I encourage you to be open and honest with yourself, and reflect deeply on your responses. Your valuable insights gained from this learning can provide you with a road map to conduct your next chalking the field conversation.

- Coaching is . . . _____

_____

_____

- When I am aware that I have a coaching situation with another person, I usually . . . _____

_____

_____

- Some things I would not do even though they help me in a coaching situation are . . . _____

_____

_____

- The best thing that can come out of a coaching situation is . . . _____

_____

_____

- A specific time when I felt good about coaching another person was when . . . _____

_____

_____

- I feel most vulnerable during a one-on-one conversation when . . . _____

_____

_____

- When involved in a one-on-one conversation with an employee, I resent it when . . . _____

_____

_____

- My greatest strength in coaching employees is . . . _____

_____

_____

- When things are going well in a coaching situation and a disagreement arises, I tend to . . . _____

  _____

  _____

- I usually hide or camouflage my feelings when . . . _____

  _____

  _____

- My greatest personal challenge in coaching effectively is . . ._____

  _____

  _____

- Six months from now I would like to be able to is . . . ____

  _____

  _____

Well, how did it go? You have just taken one of the most critical steps in the process of becoming a coach. As coach, each conversation you have with a team member helps shape the boundaries and expectations of your relationship. Great coaches take time and pride in preparing for and conducting these field-chalking dialogues. I invite you to consider the possibilities for being in relationships with others that are mutually empowering and inspiring, as you set out to chalk the field for successful individual and team performance.

7

The Language of Coaching
What It Really Means to Walk the Talk

Have you ever had the feeling that, at times, what people say is not always what they mean? For whatever reason, for some of us, saying what is on our minds and in our hearts is tough! The obvious question is why, but, unfortunately, there is not always an obvious answer. The temptation for the naive manager is to fix blame on the individual who is experiencing the inability to communicate clearly—to blame the person because he or she just can't say it. This is a limiting explanation and in fact leads to communication breakdown between the individual and manager. Then the managerial relationship with the employee can be lost.

The language of coaching doesn't have to be a foreign language for managers. Instead, with willingness to be open to learning and trying things out, today's business coach can achieve great impact with others in the new work environment.

One alternative for the manager is to approach the employee with coaching in the situation—and specifically the language of coaching—as a skill to be used to engage the conversation in a proactive way instead of causing defenses to go up. The anchor of integrity here is this notion of intentionality, or the coach's mind-set as he or she begins the dialogue process. At the very center of this mind-set is the idea of being very curious as to where the other person is coming from—suspending judgment on what is being said and instead challenging oneself to tune in to the complete message. What do I mean by complete message?

Behavioral psychologists tell us that as humans speak both fact and fiction. It is important for the coach to hear what is being said and to pick up on the nonverbal body language as well. These are components of the complete message. It takes being present and clear with yourself to allow the complete message to come through.

It has been well documented that 93% of all communication is nonverbal, leaving only 7% as the actual words in the communication process. Often, managers can be blind to this fact—the communication underneath the words. The net result is ignoring what is really important to the other person and instead blasting ahead on previous agendas and completely bypassing the opportunity to connect with the person you are trying to coach.

Connecting with team members is key to the fulfillment of *being* a successful coach. A driver of this blindness on the part of some would-be coaches is the subconscious attitude of approaching the world with an "I've got it all figured out" perspective, which greatly limits connectivity with others. When we live this way, it's almost as obvious as walking around with a neon billboard on our head for others to see, but are most of the time we completely blind to how we are coming across.

Amazing as it may seem, the "ahas" that result when the blinders are removed are remarkable for many. I can speak firsthand about this, because I was shown the light by my coach. She greatly assisted me in recognizing there are multitudes of ways to get the desired outcome. It doesn't always have to be my way. I was fortunate; the coach was my spouse and she shared this bit of coaching in a note.

Jim, you talk about you and me being a team and working together as teammates in parenting and matters of our family. You want us to be a team, but only on your terms. You want my opinion-input, but only when you ask for it. I get the feeling that the only person on your team is you! I don't want to be on that kind of team; I want to be on a team where there really is teamwork. Please let me know how you feel. Vicki.

Well, I laughed and cried. That was powerful feedback, and it made a point. Vicki revealed my blind spot that I couldn't see. When I got over the tremors of this shock, I realized that this was not a put-down, a personal attack, or a judgment; rather, it was spoken from the heart. The motive was not born out of spite or a personal vendetta—quite the opposite. She loved me (cared) enough to tell me the truth so I could have an "aha" and join the team. I believe the intent of this coaching was one of support, of midcourse correction, of getting back on the same page together and telling the truth from a caring, proactive perspective.

Now, I could have heard a completely different message and gone ballistic. My reaction could have been to dig in, fight back, get angry, argue, question Vicki's intent, and guess at what were her hidden issues. But, because her past behaviors were aligned with current behaviors and we had trust with each other, I could move beyond my fears and operate from a different mode.

What I learned from my dedicated coach (spouse) was to take off my blinders. We have the component of trust and mutual commitment, with tools to get back on the same page.

She challenged me to "walk my talk" and to understand what it really means as well as to see what I didn't know and couldn't see before. In the business world, and in the new work environment we can find ourselves coaching. It can be a critical managerial competence that will better enable us to manage conflict and resolve differences with fewer hassles. What shift is required? A shift from a controlling style to a coaching style of language. It has been said, "Your heart knows things your mind cannot."

There is much about others we will never know in the greater design of life. Perhaps it was meant to be that way. However, great coaches have mastered the ability to get to the heart of the matter with people while at the same time preserving the dignity of the individuals they are coaching.

Being a coach from the inside out means the coach has much more awareness and sensitivity for using the appropriate language. Thus, with more awareness comes a greater variety of options. If you lack the awareness, options are not as plentiful.

Visualize for a moment a recent tough coaching or communication situation you found yourself engaged in. Take a moment to outline in your mind's eye this scenario.

> What happened? How did you and the other person get to the place you are now currently in?
>
> How did your intentionality play into the relationship?
>
> What, if anything, could you have done differently that might have added a new option or alternative to the outcome?
>
> Inside this relationship, what signals may have there been about the level of mutual trust, openness, and flexibility that you might have seen had you been looking for them?

The answers to these questions, if one is honest in seeking them, will provide opportunities to learn from your behaviors and to find new strategies for coaching others. This is part of the new learning that goes along with the new work environment. It is not always easy to learn. But, when you raise your awareness and look at old situations from new perspectives, suspending all judgments, solutions will develop in new ways. If you choose to be a coach, life suddenly takes on new meaning, challenges, and opportunities to enhance the lives of yourself and others.

Today's managers, navigating the often murky waters of change and uncertainty, must rely on both the tools of navigation—compass, charts, maps—and their own internal guidance systems of intuition and heartfelt feelings about truly being of support to those they are coaching. Are you ready to create this opening in your life? I was strongly influenced by a wise teacher and practitioner of organizational development named Harvey Hornstein, the former chairman of the psychology department at Teachers College of Columbia University. He explained to me that creating a successful practice in organizational development consulting was like having a series of ongoing conversations with clients—assessing and understanding their situations, goals, needs, and desired outcomes.

I believe that is what inside-out coaches do well. They have deep and meaningful conversations, with a developmental game plan in mind. This game plan is based on current situations, assessments, data collection, and the competence/ability of the person being coached. The coach creates with the player a mutually acceptable plan of action to move from the current situation to the desired future state or outcome. This conversations include specific tactical plans, time lines, performance measurements, and standards for achieving or not achieving results.

The language of coaching is about building bridges with others and not barriers. It is about being direct and laser-clear, yet with a balance of compassion, care, and empathy for the person being coached. One of my favorite examples of this competence was demonstrated by Peter Falk in his television role as Lieutenant Columbo.

The faithful viewer knew that the detective would ultimately solve the case, but the dilemma confronting Columbo always required his ability to step back, see what was going on, assess the facts, and then plan a strategy to lead the bad guy into being caught. The signature of Columbo's success, for me, was the way he would apologetically arrest his suspects and treat even the most ruthless culprits with a certain dignity and regard, knowing full well the consequences they would face for their actions.

The skills of probing, listening, reflecting, and attending to others are core skills in the coach's tool kit of communication skills and the language of coaching.

In her book *I Wish I'd Said That!*, Linda McCallister writes:

> Communication style is concerned with how you say what you say.... People do not respond to what is said, the actual words; rather they respond to how something is said, the style or manner in which the words are used.

This is a very powerful insight when combined with the idea of intentionality. The coach can avoid the trap of being seen as a manipulator who is out solely for personal gain, willing to say whatever the person wants to hear to get it. Unfortunately, too many managers are blind to this aspect of language and cause numerous breakdowns in relationships. Far more is seen about their selfish intentions than they realize. Another language trap to be avoided is to assume that everybody communicates "just like me" and then, when the other person does not live up to expectations, to feel let down. Do you fall prey to or express either of these traps?

When you shift to even more successful coaching practices you are no longer bound solely by the traditional approach of managing (i.e., you are not locked in the belief that as manager you should know the answer and then give out the solution). A key is to remain curious about what's going on and actively seek out those opportunities to better understand observable behaviors, actions, results, and overall performance. *You can do it*!

Now you are armed with curiosity and willingness to explore the unknown. When you plunge deeper beyond the surface of issues with those you are coaching, you gain a broader, more complete picture of what is going on and become more effective.

The real significance of this coaching mind-set is that the manager is now better positioned to accurately diagnose the true problem and prescribe practices in a way that aligns with the symptoms that are presented. *Seeing through the lens of the person to be coached is key.* The metaphor that comes to mind is a pair of binoculars.

As one looks through the binoculars and adjusts the lens, the object that is being viewed comes into sharper, clearer focus until finally, with all the proper adjustments, the image is crystal clear! This focus is imperative, just as with any new skill, attitude, or knowledge, so it can be integrated into what is already known.

What does it mean to *be* a coach? The coach is always learning to apply the appropriate language of coaching, while at the same time being willing to let go of some prior interpretations of things, so that new options are created. Let me share an example.

Wally was head of the operations and service department of a large Midwestern auto dealership program. With over 22 years of experience, he believed he had seen about every service problem and operations issue imaginable. If by chance he hadn't, he would bluster his way through the conversation, making others believe he knew what the hell he was talking about even though he really didn't.

There was a little gray area in Wally's world and everybody knew it except Wally. He had been operating like this for so long—pushing people around, bullying them in meetings, yelling at customers, telling others they didn't know what they were talking about—that he was the root cause of a number of service managers quitting. Of course, Wally was always there with the reason "why so-and-so didn't work out."

In his mind, he was never part of the problem; therefore, it was difficult for him to be part of the solution.

One day, all that changed when Herb, one of Wally's long-term suppliers, had a heart attack. Wally made several visits to the hospital and one evening, after his associate was back on the road to recovery, the conversation shifted to Herb's "big wake-up call" about living and mending long-term abuses in his life.

Herb was a lot like Wally; perhaps that is why they had hit it off so well and become friends. As Herb lay in his hospital bed, reciting the numerous lessons that had flashed through his mind about the mistreatment of friends, customers, peers, and coworkers, the lightbulb went on in Wally's mind: *What if this were me?*

Almost as if he were transformed into Mr. Scrooge, Wally decided he must change.

He would have to rethink many of his favorite approaches to dealing with people. His current internal comfort zone would need to be redefined. Wally would need to unlearn a host of derailing behaviors and annoying habits. He would need to cut loose the safety net of pat answers and definitions that for so long had provided security, knowledge, power, prestige, and fulfillment.

How would he do it? Who would help him? Who could he turn to? Who could he trust? Wally found himself asking the very questions we all ask ourselves when we seek out our own coach to assist us in our development.

Then he turned back to his longtime friend, alerted by a major wake-up call and needing to act on his new awareness. *Wally discovered his coach and the coach discovered himself as a coach.* They realized they could help each other as beings of transformation through this mutual "aha." Herb and Wally made a covenant to coach one another.

What if you were coming from a similar perspective, waiting for your "aha"? You do not need a heart attack for a wake-up call like Herb did to learn to shift the language of coaching into a working formula. *You have the luxury of choosing today, in small sincere ways, to communicate more effectively as a coach.*

Our interpretation of interpersonal communication helps shape how effective we are in our relationships with others. As was the case in the Chapter 5 about turbulence and our reaction to it, the internal commotion and chaos we experience as a result of life's circumstances gets played out in our inability to choose language as a coach.

Hyler Bracey, coauthor of *Managing from the Heart*, makes a wonderful observation: *not to make people wrong* as a result of feedback and critique of their performance, ideas, thinking, or work. It makes perfectly sound sense, given all we have to go through sometimes just to get the job done.

We don't need or want to appreciate a boss, peer, or fellow worker for telling us how wrong we are. We expect straight and direct feedback about how we are doing and in a manner that focuses on the results or performance. Attacking the person does not empower or improve performance. Yet even though managers attend seminars, participate in workshops, and read all the contemporary literature on performance management, many ignore the advice of the professionals and deploy language that undermines trust building. Granted, there are those times and situations that summon all the managerial courage and forthrightness one can muster in order to confront poor performance, plus results or behaviors that are below expectations.

It is the weighed combination of managing and coaching that produces a more proactive communication style that can offer more success.

The receiver of the message pays more attention to how it's conveyed than to the actual words used. The coach must not destroy the inner spirit of the person being coached. This spirit can take the form of decision making, risk taking, self-initiative, and self-reliance; also, accountability, responsibility, and, ultimately, commitment. Are we the result of routine butt kicking and in-your-face tactics? Managers turned coaches who go into tantrums are unwelcome as not being true coaches from the inside out. Do you know any would-be coaches who operate like this?

The reality in business today is that business units have selected high-potential, bright future stars of the organization to manage their workers. However, workers may possess more experience, industry knowledge, and overall business savvy. This can be a difficult challenge for those who are charged to lead them.

The kind of language we are talking about allows managers to learn and adopt new coaching practices as tactical means, enhancing their own careers and improving the performance of others. The adage "go slow to go fast" is applicable here.

There are times when coaches get emotional, intense, angry, and very direct, but they can also manage their responses and the internal interpretation of the situation. Thus, communication style does not overshadow the intended message with an opposite message. This appears on the surface as common sense and easy to do. In this chapter's Application Exercises, I invite you to assess your own skills through an inventory to see how well you deploy this type of thinking as a natural step to relating and communicating with others.

I attended a meeting of a retailer of fashion merchandise and home furnishings, a company that had significant challenges in front of it in order to remain competitive. The senior vice president of marketing and sales gave all 700 attendees a white T-shirt with the following inscription on it:

> *If you can imagine it—you can possess it*
> *If you can dream it—you can become it*
> *If you can envision it—you can attain it*
> *If you can picture it   you can achieve it*

The sales associates turned in a record year, and there was much more to the total effort and support than just a few motivational words on a T-shirt. But, the point is that we all must start somewhere. As I mentioned earlier, it's not where you start that's important; rather, it's where you end up that is important.

Consider for a moment the opportunity that you now possess to further enhance coaching competence and mastery at using the language of coaching. Carylee Kensler, a trainer and communication expert, shared with me the following model around the notion of creating boundaries with others, instead of barriers in relationships.

As humans we all have tendencies to operate out of our own internal comfort zones. We know these are learned behaviors, and over time if they don't serve us well, they can be unlearned.

Barriers tend to be kept secret and silent in the mind of a person. They are seldom, if ever, discussed, yet we act on them as decision screens and judgmental tools in evaluating the observed behavior of others or by the person who creates barriers.

What happens is a breakdown in trust and mutual respect. After the fact, the owner of the barrier proceeds to confront the other person, who unknowingly broke the barrier. This is crucial, because as long as the owner of the barrier is unwilling to share and openly discuss why this is a barrier for them, breakdowns in communication will continue to be the norm rather than the exception in the relationship.

To compound matters, there are even some owners of barriers who fail to acknowledge to the other person that he or she just crossed the line and invaded a private area. This form of behavior as a method of communication is particularly dangerous, because you never know where the barriers are with the barrier owner.

The powerful news, according to Kensler, is that "one can change the game from keeping barriers to creating clear boundaries with others."

Boundaries are healthy; they are okay. Although they in fact represent the same issues for the boundary maker as the barrier did, because they are out in the open, exposed and negotiable, they are discussable. The other person in the relationship does not have to agree with the boundary, but can, in the spirit of mutuality in relationship, live with and abide by agreed-upon boundaries; or, if he or she crosses over the boundary, renegotiations can be discussed.

The outcome, Kensler says, offers "inclusion of the other" rather than traps, exclusion, breakdowns in communication, and someone continually being set up to fail. "Boundaries therefore create a foundation of mutual respect, understanding, need fulfillment and open communication." Boundaries create chalking the field together.

As you consider your communication options with others inside the coaching relationship, you can create for yourself many alternatives by appropriately using the language of coaching.

Now, as we come to the end of this chapter, take a few private moments and complete the Application Exercises on the following pages. Unlike the prior exercises, these ones will ask you to take a deeper view of your beliefs and actions as a coach. But like the previous exercises, these present you with the real-world opportunity to try out new thinking and attitudes in your own private gymnasium of learning.

Here is an opportunity to test some of your assumptions about communicating with others. Read each item and rate whether this is true about you. Then, review your answers and look for insights that might offer clues as to areas that you may want to improve in.

COMMUNICATION SKILLS—SELF-INVENTORY #5

- Overall, in various settings, do I consider myself as very open, honest, and straightforward with people? Yes_____ No_____

- Do I tend to guard my feelings closely, hardly ever letting others really know how I feel or think about the subject at hand? Yes_____ No_____

- Do I tend to be very open with my feelings, opinions, and beliefs regardless of whom I am speaking with or the subject of the conversation? Yes_____ No_____

- If I don't like what the other person is saying do I tend to discount it, ignore it, argue about it, mentally take a vacation, interrupt, change the subject, or none of the above since I have my own favorite instead? Yes_____ No_____

- If I am really troubled or bothered by something another person says or does to me, do I tell that person directly about how it's affecting me and what I would like instead? Yes_____ No_____

- In order not to ruffle feathers do I find some other means of managing differences with others? Yes_____ No_____

- Do I have a high level of patience with people? Am I willing to hang in there, even though it may be a little frustrating getting to the point? Yes_____ No_____

- Do I enjoy the mental and verbal combat of the give-and-take of differences in communication? Is my style to give it right back to them?   Yes_____   No_____

- Do I believe it is the politically correct thing to listen to others, but I frankly get bored easily and either go along or drift off into my own world of priorities? Yes_____   No_____

- Do I like the art of persuasion and the ability to sell or influence others to see it my way?   Yes_____   No_____

- Sometimes do I wish the other person would just shut up and quit talking so I could say my two cents worth? Yes_____   No_____

- At times do I not say what I am really thinking for fear the other person may not like me or accept me or may think I am dumb?   Yes_____   No_____

- Do I tend to get defensive when I hear things I don't like or that I disagree with?   Yes_____   No_____

- Do I pretend to agree with another person, knowing full well deep inside I don't agree at all?   Yes_____   No_____

- Do I tell the others just what they want to hear because I don't want to deal with them and their feelings? Yes_____   No_____

- Do I "tell it like it is"? Do I believe it's better to put things on the table rather than to hide them for later? Yes_____   No_____

GETTING FEEDBACK

Reflect on those areas of communication with others that you are most satisfied with:

1. What are you doing to build trust and connect with others?

2. What nonverbal signals are contrary to those situations where you have built trust, sensed clarity and purpose, and gained commitment to action from others?

3. When things didn't go well, what in your mind caused the breakdown of trust, relationship, or communication?

4. Having read this chapter, what new approaches, beliefs, or testing of current assumptions regarding the language of coaching might you choose to work on?

5. What practices could you put in place for yourself that will ensure you do not make others feel wrong, dumb, or ashamed when you are coaching?

Well, how did you do? What new options might you now be in a better position to create for yourself by using the language of coaching? Did you discover that there are some times when you are more open and vulnerable with others?

You might choose to develop the ability to better communicate about expected performance. Or, possibly, you may wish to get more comfortable managing differences. Take confidence in the fact that we are discussing learning new behaviors, skills, and attitudes, or unlearning old ones that no longer serve us. Whatever you ardently desire, vividly imagine, and enthusiastically act upon will come to be! Go forward and become the coach you wish to be.

8

Coach the Coach

Strategies for Coaching
Up and Across

Coaching can come from a variety of sources. Sometimes the coaching may be from a friend or colleague. Or, perhaps you as a coach may find yourself in the unique position of even coaching your boss. This last context of coaching has been referred to as "managing up." Whatever the situation, when you find yourself in the unique role as coach, you have the opportunity to influence the thinking, behavior, and actions of the person who is seeking coaching from you. This is no light responsibility, and if conducted properly it sets in motion a series of events that can have dramatic impact on the relationship of coach and coachee.

This chapter is about those unconventional applications and approaches to coaching where at times you as a peer or colleague find yourself in the position to offer coaching. Whether you are seeking out a coach or you have been asked to provide coaching, there must be an acknowledgement of trust in the relationship. The task now as a coach is to assist the other person, to the best of your abilities, to reach his or her desired goal.

It is important to remember that if we simply keep enacting our current world with the same interpretations (practices, thinking, and behavior) we keep the same internal comfort zone, unfortunately never reaching our full potential.

What is required then, if we truly desire to improve and to raise the level of performance to some new higher standard, is a shift in the very practices that we implement every day. We all have our favorite set of predetermined solutions as to how we see the world. Of course, we apply these visions to the various life settings we encounter in an attempt to fix our problem and lower our internal uncomfortable feelings. *It is at this exact moment that the peer coach or fellow employee coach can play such vital role for his or her friend, peer, or colleague.*

As I stated before, coaches enjoy the unique perspective of being able to see things that the persons being coached cannot see themselves. An opening is created for the coach to propose practices that then enable the other person to alter his or her current interpretations of the world. Looking through the lens of the coach, an individual is able to see new possibilities that did not exist before coaching.

This breakthrough often requires a break with some past, belief, or habit. Often we suffer and anguish over the struggle of giving up and letting go of a behavior, attitude, or time-honored belief. But the coach can both help confront the reality of ready-made solutions and reveal how they are no longer appropriate. Everyone learns that sometimes you just have to replace old approaches with new and better ones.

In friendships, these kinds of discussions go on all the time, and more likely than not they are not thought of as coaching per se. But that is exactly what they are. The fact is that with a friend, because of breadth of trust and openness in the relationship, it is easier to make the first move to seek coaching from the other. What transpires next is a series of conversations around possible actions that the individual seeking coaching might take to resolve the issues.

Work relationships are not that much different from personal relationships, once the foundation of trust has been built. When trust is high, communication flows freely and endlessly. The elements of trust—being reliable, speaking the truth, being open with others, and accepting and appreciating others while demonstrating competence—are all learnable attitudes and behaviors. Situations at work with coworkers or even bosses where the ingredients of trust exist offer the possibility for authentic coaching to take place.

The coaching diagram in Figure 8-1 illustrates graphically the opportunity for coaching. Inside any relationship there is a "point of entry" by the coach, peer, or coworker when one can enter the relationship as a coach. As in any form of coaching, this opening, or entry point, can be a result of what the coach has done to encourage the other person to seek out the coach. It becomes obvious from past consistent behaviors and actions that a "coachable moment" has just been created. Now the coach can offer coaching under favorable conditions with a high level of receptivity by the individual being coached.

This activity can be seen all the time in the growth of a relationship between a new employee and a supervisor, or between two peers who are creating a trusting relationship. The film *Working Girl* portrays a classic example.

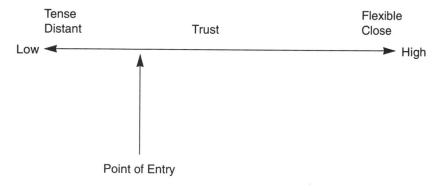

Figure 8-1 *Inside the coaching relationship.*

Over time, the character played by Harrison Ford encourages a secretary (Melanie Griffith) to pursue her own dreams and goals while overcoming limitations that are self-imposed. These are beliefs about work, performance, success, and self. In a memorable scene when Griffith looks to Ford to solve her problem, he literally lets her go, pushes her out to soar on her own to reach new heights.

You will notice that at one end of the continuum of relationships the relationship might be tense, closed, and distant, with communication awkward and difficult. At the other end, trust is high, there is a sense of mutuality in the relationship, communication is easy, and you get second chances to overcome mistakes.

Planning questions cause you, the coach, to analyze where you are in the relationship and what is your point of entry. *What is the history (if any) between the other person and you? What goals do you as well as the other person have? What potential barriers exist inside the relationship?* These can help you, the coach, develop an appropriate game plan for coaching a friend, peer, coworker, or even your boss!

Now, let's have you think about creating a real-world application for yourself to practice with. Follow the process and work through a current coaching opportunity with which you are involved.

Perhaps the following peer coaching in a business situation will be helpful to illustrate the possibilities of coaching between two team leaders.

Brit was a talented mechanical/design engineer. Not only did she possess excellent individual competencies to perform her job, but she also understood team involvement. Brit excelled both academically and athletically while she was at Stanford University. She now found herself in the envious position of fast-tracking through the organization in her business career.

Having contributed greatly on two project teams, Brit had been promoted to team leader of the new product development group on a government contract to design and produce state-of-the-art jet airplanes. Her new assignment called for her to be a coach to the project team and team members.

Her first instinct was to fall back on the role models she had as a Division One soccer player as well as other coaching experiences she had encountered. The problem was, those lessons were not helping her much now.

The single biggest headache Brit was experiencing, she confided in Dawn, a fellow team leader who was also on the fast track and a high-potential path, was that the other people on her team were "not on the same wavelength." They didn't possess the same inner moves, the sense of when to act or how to anticipate and flow with the rhythm of the project. Brit and Dawn discussed the differences between coaching a team and being the star player.

Dawn had grasped the differences early in her shift from outstanding individual contributor to team leader. Brit, on the other hand, struggled making her transition because she relied so heavily on her own intuitive savvy and individual strengths and was not able to capitalize on the multiple talents of her team.

Dawn explained to Brit, "The ironic thing is, Brit, the more you press to use power, sheer strength, and self-reliance on solving perceived problems, the more limited you are."

Instead of seeing possibilities in others, Brit was totally focused on herself to the detriment of the team. Her coaching efforts were now seen as moves to control others, to take credit where it should have been given, to drive an agenda that was viewed as selfish and one-sided. This might have been avoided if Brit realized what *being* a coach was about instead of trying to *act like* one.

Dawn, as a peer coach, could talk with Brit both as a peer and as a coach. Dawn could influence the attitude and behavior of Brit, while adding value to Brit's efforts at being a coach to her project team. The peer coaching was genuine and supportive while also being direct, to the point, and honest. Dawn was able to help Brit see possibilities she was blind to. Dawn helped raise Brit's game to a higher level.

Dawn had participated in a coaching course I had conducted at her company. One of the take-away tools we used was an exercise that helps the coach speak the truth to the other person. It preserves the dignity and integrity of coach, peer, friend, and coworker by focusing on the observed behavior, not the person.

This planning process is here for you to use (see Application Exercises). It creates the possibility of allowing the coach to learn and be coachable, from what is said and not said, and why.

When your intent is honorable and trustworthy, you can be honest in communicating behavior and performance.

You may desire to try the Application Exercises out as a means to coaching a peer, friend, or coworker, or even in coaching your boss.

INSIDE THE COACHING RELATIONSHIP

1. In the coaching relationship illustrated in Figure 8-1, what do you expect to happen?

2. Describe your current relationship with this person (i.e., key elements).

   History._____

   Expectations. _____

   Performance issues. _____

   Level of trust._____

   Communication._____

   Points of resistance/conflicts._____

DESIRED OUTCOMES

1. What do you want from this relationship?_____
   _____

2. What current or possible barriers stand in the way of achieving your goals with this individual? _____
   _____

3. Create a game plan: What are your options here, given what you know about the relationship?_____
   _____

4. Having assessed this situation and relationship, what coaching might you use for yourself? What new possibilities emerged for you (if any)?_____
   _____

Well, how did you do? What did you learn about yourself as a coach, the other person you are coaching, and the overall coaching relationship?

IMAGERY—COACHING SITUATION

Think about a recent or near future coaching situation you are or will be involved in. Complete the following:

1. Briefly describe the situation: _____

    _____

2. What are (were) your objectives?_____

    _____

3. How did you plan for the conversation? _____

    _____

4. What happened as a result of the coaching? _____

    _____

The work and writings of Chris Argyros, professor emeritus of Harvard Business School and the Harvard Graduate School of Education, have prompted me to develop the following coaching tool for peer coaching.

COACHING DEBRIEFING RECORD FOR PEER COACHING

As you review your coaching conversation, write out the conversation as you recall it in the first column. In the second column, write what you left out—what you didn't say. Compare the two columns and look for differences.

What You Actually Said	What You Didn't Say, but Perhaps Wish You Had
_____	_____
_____	_____
_____	_____
_____	_____
_____	_____

1. What prevented you from conveying your complete thoughts, feelings, and so forth? _____

2. How might you have been able to express yourself more fully, while avoiding attacking or accusing the other person or personalizing the situation? _____

3. Having had this conversation, where are you today with this person? _____

4. What are possible next steps to improve and enhance your communication with this person? _____

This returns us to the importance of understanding and working with your intentionality in coaching (Chapter 2). I encourage and support you in applying these concepts to coaching peers, coworkers, friends, and even your boss.

FOCUS GROUP COMMENTS FOR PEER COACHING

I was working with the back-office support staff of a financial trading company when various staffers listed the following attributes for successfully coaching each other at work.

- Superior performance in getting people aligned with the overall purpose.
- Listening and providing a supportive environment.
- Consistency in coaching at all times, at all levels.
- Strong communication skills.

Other comments:

- Different teams exist; opportunities for coaching are different.
- Key words for an outstanding coach are: developer, healer.
- I believe our company supports empowerment.
- Building relationships over time exists in the sports world; it is now beginning to become a reality in the business world.
- We need to be able to recognize change in behavior by employees.
- How do we improve performance, overcome wishful thinking, and be proactive as a coach?
- We need to have an objective of the game so we can coach to results.
- Employees must witness coaching behaviors to believe they are true.

A coach is a . . .

- Developer.
- Healer.
- Teacher.
- Mentor
- Respecter of other people.

- Role model.
- Team builder.
- Leader to give recognition to others.
- Learner.

A coach . . .

- Listens well.
- Gives feedback.
- Is compassionate.
- Creates opportunities to share information.
- Keeps on focus.
- Provides positive attitudes.
- Is consistent with all levels.
- Gives positive reinforcement.
- Shares experiences and perspectives.
- Serves the needs of others.

The purpose of working with this organization was to create a coaching process for the business that would enable staff and supervisors to have a mutually understood process to coach one another.

We created a four-step process that is outlined in Figure 8-2. The process begins with the peer coach having a supportive attitude; a developmental perspective follows, with an attitude of collaboratively resolving issues, affirming confidence of the peer to achieve his or her goals.

For each of the circles (Figures 8-3 through 8-6), there is a list of factors that contribute to, or help define the title of the circle (support, development, resolve, affirmation).

Next, there is a set of questions for each step that peers, friends, or coworkers might ask themselves in order to as-

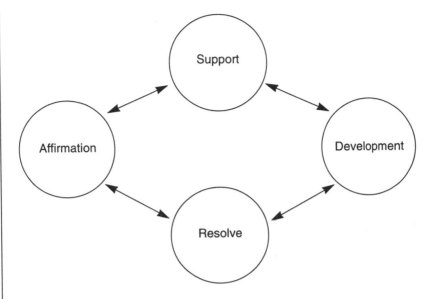

Figure 8-2 *Four-step coaching process.*

sess how well the coach demonstrates the behaviors listed in the circle.

This is an important aid in the coaching process because it creates the opportunity for both coach and those being coached to assess how the coach is doing.

COACHING VALUE QUESTIONS

Support Circle

- Does my coach feel comfortable during a coaching session? Does my coach build trust and listen to me? Is my coach sincere?

- Does my coach take an appropriate amount of time to cover the subject with me. Is my coach clear, firm, and direct, without attacking or putting me down or making me feel dumb?

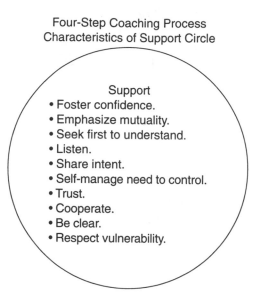

Four-Step Coaching Process
Characteristics of Support Circle

Support
• Foster confidence.
• Emphasize mutuality.
• Seek first to understand.
• Listen.
• Share intent.
• Self-manage need to control.
• Trust.
• Cooperate.
• Be clear.
• Respect vulnerability.

Figure 8-3 *Support circle—a set of descriptions for being supportive in the coaching context.*

- Does my coach help me deal with barriers or obstacles that stand in the way of my action plans?
- Does my coach help me understand and overcome reservations, fears, or resistance regarding change or new approaches?
- Does my coach demonstrate true concern and interest in my development and unique needs?

Development Circle

- Does my coach help me fully understand the size, scope, and shape of areas to be developed?
- Does my coach help me anticipate the future effects of the action plan on others and relate the impact of what we are trying to do clearly?
- Does my coach help me expand my thinking beyond what I see, help me uncover blind spots, and help me relate the unrelated?

Four-Step Coaching Process
Characteristics of Development Circle

Development
• Chalk the field.
• Communicate expectations.
• Improve competence.
• Assess strengths, weaknesses.
• Create climate.
• Engineer coachability.

Figure 8-4 *Development circle—a set of descriptions for guiding development in the coaching context.*

• Does my coach provide specific and timely feedback on my developmental efforts?

• Does my coach encourage me to take a personal initiative to create new innovative approaches and responsibility for my continuous improvement?

Resolve Circle

• Does my coach fully explore the future positive and negative outlooks of my performance or lack of performance?

• Does my coach express and follow through on the coach's own personal commitments and plans for change?

• Does my coach accept some responsibility when plans, actions, or assignments do not turn out as expected?

• Does my coach recognize the role the coach plays in my development and need for improvement by listening to and accepting feedback?

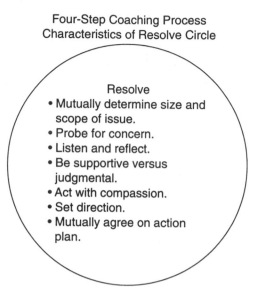

Four-Step Coaching Process
Characteristics of Resolve Circle

Resolve
• Mutually determine size and
  scope of issue.
• Probe for concern.
• Listen and reflect.
• Be supportive versus
  judgmental.
• Act with compassion.
• Set direction.
• Mutually agree on action
  plan.

Figure 8-5 *Resolve circle—a set of descriptions for issue resolution in the coaching context.*

- Does my coach help me clearly understand how and where I am accountable and responsible, and how I will be measured for my efforts?

Affirmation Circle

- Does my coach show strong commitment to my success by expressing confidence in my abilities?

- Does my coach help me build competence and be self-correcting and self-generating?

- Does my coach control own emotions, like anger or frustration, and give me a clear message of wanting to hear me out when I express my opinions?

- Does my coach hold me accountable for results, but not micromanage or "shrink the boundaries" of what is possible for me to initiate and take action on?

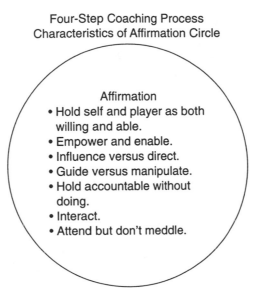

Four-Step Coaching Process
Characteristics of Affirmation Circle

Affirmation
• Hold self and player as both willing and able.
• Empower and enable.
• Influence versus direct.
• Guide versus manipulate.
• Hold accountable without doing.
• Interact.
• Attend but don't meddle.

Figure 8-6 *Affirmation circle—a set of descriptions for being affirmative and accountable in the coaching context.*

• Does my coach promote an atmosphere of honest, open communication by sharing information and conducting sensitive, demanding conversation?

The most encouraging and empowering lesson I learned by working on the concept of coaching the coach is that with ongoing practice the coach can learn effectively to develop a set of appropriate behaviors that support coaching the coach.

In the next Application Exercise, you have the opportunity to individually reflect deeply about your beliefs and actions in coaching the coach in business. As in the preceding exercises, I invite you to continue your own self-discovery as a coach, and to learn from the insights you gain by examining your life experiences.

As you think about possible peer, coworker, friend, or even boss coaching situations, you might find this exercise helpful.

Consider a time in recent history, in either your business or personal life, where as a peer, coworker, or friend you were the coach or you sought some coaching.

- What made this coaching special, significant, and valuable?

- What was your intent in the role?

- How did your intent affect the coaching outcome?

- In your future coaching as a peer, coworker, or friend, what could you do to enhance your coaching and overall relationship with those you are coaching?

9

Getting in Shape
A Workout for a Coach in Training

Life sometimes leads us through twists, turns, ups and downs, for no apparent reason and often against our will. Change surrounds us, it confounds us, and it can debilitate us. Or, we can learn to thrive in a world of rapid and turbulent thrusts of change.

It was somehow odd that as I began work on this chapter what I had set out to do with the book, help others learn to be better business coaches, became paramount for applying these lessons to coach myself. Throughout the book we have been describing this new work environment and what it takes to thrive in it as a coach. Suddenly, without apparent warning, I found myself a victim of the infamous corporate downsizing.

Actually, my experience also took on a whole ethical dimension. The company published a business code of conduct, and I found myself raising questions about a questionable set of behaviors to my superiors, looking for guidance. Unfortunately, the timing of a corporate restructuring and an ethical question left me out on the street. Frankly, had I deployed the range of skills, competencies, and awarenesses that we have been discussing so far, I might well have been able to detect the turbulence just over the horizon. They say to look for the silver lining in every cloud, and perhaps here, too, there is one.

If indeed that silver lining was a wake-up call for me to remain ever vigilant in the ongoing and regular updating of my own self-development and to "walk my talk," I got the message.

What I was soon confronted with were some monstrous questions and challenges. *Why did this happen to me? What do I do now? Where do I go next? How will I survive?* Thankfully I was in a place and time where I could function as a coach to myself, as well as being able to seek out coaching from some great coaches who had helped me before.

The new work environment had just given me a whopping jolt of reality! It was as if I had been knocked way off center and I was spinning like a top, tilting from side to side. Luckily I landed on my feet doing the thing I most enjoy, helping people solve their problems, only this time for myself.

This new world of work had taught me something special: If I was to succeed I would need to become more agile, nimble, flexible, responsive—meaning I would need to fundamentally rethink my personal vision of who I wanted to be and what I was good at doing in life. All of you who have gone through this process know just what I am talking about, and those of you who have not should commit now to pursue a journey of discovering your unique purpose in life and the gifts/talents that are your offering to others.

All great coaches understand this dimension of self well. It is the core of self-awareness, confidence, humility, and self-improvement. It is the mythical training camp all great coaches go through to gain the attitudes, knowledge, and skills to excel as a coach and to raise a very fundamental question: Who coaches the coach?

This chapter is about the training camp a coach must attend in order to get him- or herself in shape to coach. World-class, championship-level athletes all train and condition themselves to reach peak performance.

After all, why should we assume that only players attend training camp? If in fact we believe that coaches must "walk the talk," then wouldn't it be true that they must learn how? Where do coaches go for coaching? What does a workout in training look like for a coach? Why must a coach continue to update his or her own competence and attitudes around coaching? How do coaches determine what areas of improvement they should continue to work on?

These are just some of the many questions coaches must address if they are in fact to remain at the top of their game.

It would be unrealistic to assume that world-class athletes would remain in peak condition if they failed to train on a regular basis, that heavyweight boxers would be able to contend for the world title if they were not fit to fight, that a basketball team would vie for the NBA championship if they had not prepared for and practiced for the grueling NBA season, or that actors/actresses would win the Academy Award if they didn't practice, rehearse, and learn their role.

Why, then, should businesses expect managers to function as coaches in business without the appropriate awareness, training, and conditioning? They shouldn't.

Here again is one of the dilemmas that confront the sports enthusiasts use of coaching and sports in business. There is no doubt and no speculation that world-class performance in the domains of sports and entertainment requires coaching, but why coaching is not fully implemented in the world of business remains for me a mystery.

Frankly, this book is not about explaining this issue or defending either side. It is more important to understand and explore how professionals in this new world of work who desire to be coaches continuously improve their skills. I do believe if you are willing to consider the practices of benchmarking and the spirit of identifying best practices in nonrelated fields, then the possibility does exist for a business coach to learn from the sports coach about how to continue to hone best practices.

Here is an example:

A company was confronted with the worst responsiveness ratings in customer service it had ever received. It was experiencing repeated breakdowns in being able to meet customers' expectations. Thus, it was losing customers, paying significantly more to attract new ones, and consistently failing to retain them.

The company managers decided that they needed to benchmark—study the best applications of firms that delivered outstanding customer service—and then look for ways to apply that learning to their own organization.

This company also chose to go outside the boundaries of traditional thinking and study the processes, systems, and practices of a world-class auto racing team with its pit crew. The managers discovered that the best in class in the field know and understand well that seconds mean the difference between winning and losing. The most responsive teams are the ones that can function together under pressure and adverse conditions. The outcome for the business by learning and applying the auto racing team's best practices in performing and responding during races led to the business team's record breakthrough responding and performing in business with their customers.

Breakthroughs are also possible for the business coach to achieve by understanding and applying some of the best practices of world-class, championship coaches in sports, entertainment, theater, and the arts. The key is for the business coach to hold open the possibility to learn from and then apply new learning on the job.

The next natural question might be, where do you go in order to find someone who knows the solutions you seek? Where do you find others who are willing to assist you in your search to become a coach and who can point out options to help solve your problems?

Those who possess the true ability to create time and space for coaching will be obvious to you. As a coach of a coach, their work takes on new meaning. They are the lights for others to follow. Perhaps a small illustration would be helpful.

Two organizational development consultants had been partners and colleagues for a short time. In their work they often traded on each other's differences, which tended to be their own individual skills that were unique to the person and of value to their client.

After a time, the "partnership romance" started to wear off as the frustration of long sales cycles began taking its toll and the partners' differences became sources of friction rather than advantages. They decided to look into coaching.

Sam was a middle-aged practitioner, full of enthusiasm and vitality. He consistently received excellent evaluations for his seminars-workshops. He was smooth and entertaining; the attendees not only got value from the sessions but also gave the workshops a high rating. It seemed that Sam had a sales personality as well. He was outgoing and persuasive, and always had a pocketful of local stories to tie the learning points into the participants' world.

Dave, on the other hand, was more of an academic; he waited for customers and potential clients to call him seeking his services. Because consulting is for the most part a relationship and referral business, this strategy is a sound one. The only caveat here is that the strategy works when the consulting practice is established and recognized as delivering value to customers.

Sam was a good consultant who understood and applied the benefits of a consulting service with his clients. He could sense the buying motives and needs of clients and could present the value of the firm's offering in a way that the potential customer would want to buy.

Sam was also proactive. He would make things happen as opposed to waiting for things to happen to him. Sam was feeling the pressure of starting a new business, and Dave's lack of urgency was beginning to get to Sam. In fact, as I began working with Sam, he had already begun being a "hot reactor."

The traditional approach for Sam in interpersonal conflict was to confront, to move forward and target the other person like an approaching panzer tank.

I prodded Sam to recognize when he was in overdrive and headed toward crushing opposition. An alternative to the aggressive attack style of coaching was for Sam to try asking questions and then listen to the answers. For example, Sam could ask Dave about what a shift in behavior might look like if Dave were to pursue consulting contracts more proactively.

Further, what action was Dave hoping the prospective customer would take, if in fact he simply waited for the phone to ring as opposed to actively pursuing the business? By getting Sam to slow down, step back, and remain curious by asking questions, I was able to *coach the coach* so that he in turn could go back and coach his partner. Sam's normal approach would have caused Dave to get defensive, withdraw from real conversation, and perhaps meekly comply with Sam's demands until the first real form of client resistance and then resort to his old behavior. The outcome instead produced a new conversation between Sam and Dave. Sam used the chalking the field concept to plan his approach and then engaged Dave in a series of conversations that got Dave to talk openly about his reluctance to actively sell their services to potential customers and to proactively seek ways of moving the ball forward toward closing business.

Sam learned more about Dave by asking questions and listening than he would have had he done all the talking. Sam and Dave ended up getting mutual commitment from each other to support one another. In the process of helping Dave learn to be more of a sales/marketing person, Sam also learned about himself as a coach.

Partly by working with me he saw opportunities for his relationship with Dave that he had not seen earlier and perhaps would have remained blind to had we not worked together. Thus, the coaching loop was closed. The coach learned more about the person he was coaching. The coaching practice itself was more effective and lasting because of this, and the coach learned to be coached himself.

Dave and Sam's relationship and business survived the turbulence, and flourished through change and transition. The coach, upon getting coached, enhanced his own performance as well as that of the person he in turn coached.

In some ways Sam was like the business team who chose to get outside their comfort zone to explore new alternatives to enhancing their performance. The workout for the coach in training begins with the proper conditioning of the mind. This means first recognizing the need for ongoing refinement of one's own coaching competence.

All human beings have a range of fears: fear of failure, embarrassment, not living up to expectations, rejection, losing respect, and not being appreciated, to name just a few. To achieve greatness as a coach, one must not cover up one's fears; rather, acknowledge them as real and seek assistance for overcoming them.

I remember designing a unique approach for a business where the leader desired shifting his business culture from one of having supervisors act like cops to one of having the manager operate as a coach. In order to create this possibility, I coached this business executive to establish a cadre of business coaching consultants from the ranks of ordinary line managers who were nominated by their peers, coworkers, and bosses to be coaches.

Of course, what made the final outcome of creating a core competency of coaching in the business a reality was that line managers were the teachers. They owned the process from one end to the other. They saw a need for learning to be coaches as part of the business strategy: being willing to learn and teach fellow supervisors coaching skills, being self-aware and corrective of their own behaviors, calling one another on breakdowns, and recognizing the true effort and achievement of all involved. They created a proven success in which a coaching culture was woven into the very fabric of the business.

The very essence of this learning plan was the coach training camp. The following guidelines for coaches in training framed the learning covenant of those line and staff managers who desired to become coaching consultants. Besides the traditional leader training that would follow, the coach, in order to be coached, needed to make a personal commitment to learn.

The true gift of coaching can be realized and applied in a relationship only when there is a state of readiness. The coach must ask for the coaching. The coach, while not acting blindly, must indeed act on the coaching given. The coach must recognize the need for coaching and self-improvement. The coach must remain open throughout the coaching process to coaching and practice. Each coach must apply the lessons learned in being a coach. Coaches must hold themselves as willing and able to be coached.

Trust the coach. Mutually participate in coaching. Don't be a passive participant. The coach must look for active ways to improve and practice coaching.

Stay open to redefining the field through experience, know-how, and changing conditions. Coaches must be 100% present in conversations with their coach as well as those they hope to coach. Create a win-win coaching relationship.

Create a trust inside the relationship of those the coach is coaching by clarifying expectations, values, possibilities, and options for improved performance. Remain curious and inquisitive about the beliefs, thoughts, and actions of those whom the coach would coach, instead of being judgmental, subjective, and controlling. Keep being self-ware and corrective in nature with coaching. Be open to learn from past mistakes and risks, while at the same time applying new learning to enhance performance.

The process of getting in shape to coach results in a shift of thinking and state of readiness as a coach. This shift also creates a different approach to interacting with people and in coaching relationships. The experience I have found in my coaching work is that this process of learning to coach is like apprenticeships in the trades. However, one significant difference in business is that often in organizations and firms there is a shortage of true masters with whom to apprentice.

My firm belief is that business has not produced large numbers of role models in coaching for others to follow. But the apprentice, if truly inspired, can find those in the organization or outside it to learn from in order to develop coaching competence. So, what is this shift in perspective that I alluded to as a result of completing the process of getting in shape to coach? Here are a few approaches to working with people, with the traditional command-and-control method on the left and the more collaborative, coaching model on the right. By the way, I am not saying that the more traditional approach has not produced results for some people in some situations. However, the current literature on business, world affairs, and the arts all support the notion that improved personal relationships as well as optimum performance are achieved through a strategy of collaboration, honoring diversity, and coaching.

Being Out of Shape to Coach	Getting in Shape to Coach
Defines the relationship narrowly: "Let me tell you how it will be."	Negotiates the coaching relationship: "Let's discuss our relationship."
"I am right."	"I see your point; tell me more about why you feel that way."
"I stick to my guns."	"Let's look at other options and alternatives."
Seeks certainty around rules, regulations, and policies. Employs tried-and-true tactics.	Accepts guidelines and policies, but also accepts uncertainty. Enjoys the conversation of creating new approaches to old patterns of thinking.
Makes statements with little wiggle room: "I am certain," "There is no doubt," "I believe this is the only solution."	Takes a more flexible stance: "It depends."
Believes in self-reliance and going it alone: "I am doing just fine here, thank you."	Asks: "How can I best relate, be a resource, be supportive?"
Tends to be blunt, straight-forward, bold: "You are wrong."	Tends to be tactful: "I want to understand."
Implements a tactic of control from a position of power to influence decision or behavior: "Do it, because I gave the order."	"How can we work this out? What can we both do to get what we want?"
Takes the nonnegotiable view: "You always know where you stand with me."	Takes a direct stand on key issues, but is willing to consider other's points of view and perspective.

If you are at all like I was when I first began this journey of learning to become a coach in business, it's easy to feel overwhelmed and discouraged at the moment of personal change and growth required to make the shift in being. But take heart in the fact that the single biggest challenge is the part you have almost completed—self-awareness!

By managing to read this far, as well as working on the Application Exercises, you are creating you own coaching game plan. As you think about what it means to be a coach and the continuous improvement path you are now on, you possess the necessary equipment by which to create the game plan of the future.

The pen, paper, thoughts, and strategies for creating a daily playbook by which you compete in your business are yours to choose. I trust you will choose well and wisely! In order to assist you in making your own decisions, please work on the following Application Exercises for this chapter.

COACHING PLANNING GUIDE FOR GETTING IN SHAPE TO
COACH

1. What elements of coaching do I now see as my strengths? Why? _____

   _____

2. How can I gather from others their views on my coaching competence? Am I willing to remain open to their feedback? _____

   _____

3. What daily or weekly practice can I design for myself that will help enable me to move toward my desired state of being a coach? _____

   _____

4. What measurement might I put in place to chart and track my progress and results? _____

   _____

5. If I were to create a powerful affirmation for myself and daily review as a coach, what would it be? _____

   _____

A colleague of mine who pitched in professional baseball and held a PGA golf card was asked, "How could a person who has been away from the game for some time go out and shoot a subpar round of golf or throw curveballs years after playing?" My associate's answer: "Muscle memory."

After years of visualizing desired outcomes and practicing the actual required muscle movements, the body internalizes the rhythm and motion required to throw strikes and hit greens consistently. This same phenomenon will apply to your development as a coach. As you develop and acquire the knowledge, skill, and competence to coach, the more effective and masterful you will become. Keep on your path of learning and creating your game plan for success.

You can build "miracle memories" for being a coach.

By following the guiding principles in coaching others that are listed below, you too can build "muscle memory" into your coaching mind-set.

COACHING GUIDING PRINCIPLES

The Coach . . .

1. Shows strong commitment to others' success by expressing confidence in others' abilities.

2. Helps others build competence and be self-correcting and, self-generating.

3. Controls own emotions, like anger or frustration, and gives others a clear message of wanting to hear them out when they express their opinions.

4. Holds others accountable for results, but does not micromanage or "shrink the boundaries" of what is possible for others to initiate and take action on.

5. Promotes an atmosphere of honest, open communication by sharing information and conducting sensitive, demanding conversation.

6. Believes in own heart and embodies in own behavior that coaching is about developing others fully.

The most encouraging and empowering aspect of getting in shape to coach is that for a manager it doesn't have to be an "impossible dream." With ongoing practice with a coach, business managers can learn to effectively shift their thinking and develop a set of appropriate behaviors that support coaching competence.

In the next Application Exercise, you have the opportunity to reflect about your beliefs, actions, and skills as a coach in business. Like the preceding exercises, this invites you to continue your own self-discovery as a coach, and to learn from the insights you gain by examining your life experiences.

As you reflect on what you need to create for yourself to become a coach, think about a time in recent history in either your business or personal life when all the elements of coaching seemed to come together in that relationship.

- What made this coaching special, significant, and valuable?

- What was your mind-set in your role?

- How did your mind-set affect the coaching outcome?

- How will what you read help your training and getting in shape to coach?

10

Preparing the
Team to Win
A Game Plan for Success

In working through my thinking on this book, I realized that there was not a more important chapter than this one, "Preparing the Team to Win."

In every book, theatrical performance, or game there is always a finale. While this may be a concluding chapter of the book, the intent is to encourage you to continue your work into the future. In fact, one may even make the case that the future is now. It's your turn to chart a new course of action as a coach. All that has gone before—the thinking, planning, adjusting, and coaching—has all been in preparation, a prelude for things to come.

True, much coaching also happens after the fact as a result of capturing and improving on lessons learned. However, coaching is always forward-thinking; it is about creating new possibilities. It is a collaborative, interactive process designed to improve the thinking, behavior, skill, and/or performance of another and open the door for future enhanced results.

The significance of this chapter is for your success as a coach as well as for those being coached. I purposely chose to address a very important issue in this chapter—the differences between coaching a team and coaching an individual.

I have said that no coach designs a game plan without a team or an individual to share it with. While called "Preparing the Team to Win," this chapter must also include preparing the individual to win.

Coaching is a one-on-one activity with players, employees, associates, or whatever the name might be for those in business being coached. Some coaches spend their whole career coaching the individual player, employee, associate, or contributor. What we have presented works nicely for both teams and individuals. However, subtle changes occur in tactics, and focus when the coaching is for the individual contributor. Some coaches in business fail to recognize these differences in coaching and thus are not successful as coaches.

The game changes when it is a sole performance, when winning or losing comes down to one individual performing not for the good of an overall team but for the individual. This is a different type of coaching and requires a different application of coaching knowledge, skills, and attitudes. It's important to remember that the spirit of coaching and the principles you have been learning and practicing are intended to be deployed inside the coaching relationship, be it the team or the individual. The sports coach understands and practices both team and individual coaching. In business, managers all to often fail to recognize the differences. That's the trouble in business coaching—the tendency to be more talk than "walking the talk."

What gets lost at times in the romance of sports coaching and in business is that 99% of the time coaching is a one-on-one relationship. An extension of coaching, then, is the relationship the coach has with individual team members as they collectively perform as a team or work group. Individuals make up the team, and the coach must be alert to relationships among team members as well as the focus for the entire team.

Throughout the book and even in the subtitle, I have attempted to make the obvious point that the world of work is changing. In the everyday occurrences of work, many of the challenges you face in your job require some form of teamwork. (You will notice I did not say "being on a team.") People across the country and around the world are being pulled together through collaboration, agreements to accomplish specific tasks, and assignments. Being able to get along, cooperate, help others, and listen more than speak are desired behaviors that most companies want employees to exhibit.

True teams are interested and committed to far more than just getting along. Powerful teams are composed of people who know and agree with the vision and purpose of the team. Further, they know and understand well their individual roles and expectations. Contributions and performance are the measurements for success. Team members hold themselves individually accountable while possessing a pervasive spirit on the team. They exhibit commitment and the attitude of doing whatever it takes to succeed.

Coaching plays a vital role in supporting both teamwork and team development. The coach is uniquely positioned to help ensure the success of the mission.

Now that you see the context for this discussion, let's return to the differences in coaching the individual performer and the team.

In coaching the individual, the significant point of departure is that the ultimate responsibility for the outcome of this situation rests squarely on the shoulders of the performer. There is no team to look to for backup. Errors and mistakes cannot be compensated for by someone else, picking up the individual's game. Performance is on the line every moment for this sole performer.

Team goals and outcomes do not determine success; rather, success is measured by the individual's accomplishments. The spotlight is always on the individual and not shared by others. Practices are designed and executed by the individual and not the team. Strategies are individual in nature and address the issues of self-reliance, mood management, single-mindedness, and mental toughness. The individual performer develops the ultimate sense of self-reliance to survive the grueling rigor of competition.

The coach of the individual performer needs to look no further than that performer for the root cause of breakdown. Corrective action is confined to the focus of the competitor, not a team. You as a coach have the added value to see possibilities that the individual may not see.

The team approach is concerned with similar issues, but the venue of competition is very different. Teams compete with other teams. All team members share winning and losing. Practice involves multiple moves, plays, and strategies, and all have to be choreographed into a unified performance. The coach must be concerned with building cohesion and agreement of all team members.

One huge difference between the team and the individual is that when breakdown occurs there is a variety of input by team members. Members' multiple solutions may occur in unpredictable ways because the team, of course, may have multiple sources of breakdown. Corrective action may well differ for various subfunctions on the team.

Thus, prevention of and solutions for breakdowns must be designed and communicated in a manner that ensures that the sum is greater than the parts. The coach of a team must plan for all the components of the team while the coach of the sole practitioner must focus on that practitioner.

No doubt coaches, like those they are coaching, feel the same pain of losing and exhilaration of winning regardless of whether a team or an individual is competing. The fundamentals of preparation and planning are shared by both kinds of coaches.

There are the same common threads of trust, communication, intentionality, and mood management in both domains of coaching.

The most important lesson here is that the coach of a team and the coach of an individual contributor have different interpretations of coaching practices. There is a difference between coaching an Olympic freestyle skier and the U.S. hockey team.

Both individual and team coaches could begin the process with their own intentionality, an ability to navigate turbulence and chalk the field, while at the same time creating an environment where trust is high and communication flows clearly with both positive and corrective feedback. But their paths separate on a tactical level, as the coach begins the process of assessing performance, seeing the holes in the game, and designing practices to move the player(s) to the next level of desired competence. The intensity of the coaching could be the same while application may vary widely.

It is a general principle in world-class sports that the higher the level of competition, the more intense the training and coaching must be. Often this does not correlate to business. Too many times people are placed in high-pressure, complex assignments without the proper training and conditioning for the job. To make matters worse, managers are not trained and coached to be coaches, so there is a double whammy!

When breakdowns occur, the manager blames the employee and the employee blames the system. Unfortunately, the real losers are ultimately the customers—both external and internal customers. Proper coaching in advance can prevent breakdowns from occurring. With a real solution in place, the likelihood of the same breakdown reoccurring is greatly reduced.

The whole question of preparing the team or individual performer to win is about the coach recognizing the type of coaching that is needed and applying the appropriate blend of knowledge, attitudes, and skills to the coaching situation.

Corey was a lead supervisor of the second shift of a manufacturing plant. He was what has been called a "players' coach," meaning that the team members had great respect for the coach as a person who related well as a human being. This quality, as well as Corey's competence of knowing the game of business and the business of coaching during the game, was what made the difference for Corey.

In business language, the people orientation is the "soft" side of management. The "hard" side, namely the financials, operations, and day-to-day running of the business, is often deemed more important by senior management. Corey had a commitment to see others succeed and grow.

> Corey was always talking up his people. He would go out regularly with them, have a beer after work, listen, and be accessible. He did a lot of the right things around the plant and on his shift. In small, consistent ways Corey was able to build trust and respect with his work group on second shift.
>
> Because he had over 40 people on his shift he knew it would be difficult to get to know them all personally, yet he worked diligently at it. He made it a priority to know everybody by first name and a little something about each one. Of course it was easier with some than others.
>
> If you walked out on the shop floor and asked the workers about how they felt and viewed Corey, you would be amazed by their reaction. It was as if each and every one of those workers had a personal relationship with their supervisor. You could feel the trust, the mood of the place. There was a commitment to both not let Corey down and not let one another down. The spirit of team was vast and deep. It was completely honest and genuine.
>
> Corey had succeeded at embedding the individual accountability for performance to high standards, while at the same time he had created incredible alignment with the team on second shift.

This story is a little different from the one portrayed in Rick Telander's *From Red Ink to Roses*. In this book from the senior writer for *Sports Illustrated*, the turbulent transformation of a Big Ten football program is chronicled and documented. For our discussion, it is interesting to compare the business case of Corey with the following story from Telander's book:

On the wall of the University of Wisconsin weight training room are these words in bright red letters, TRUST, COMMITMENT, LOVE, BELIEF. These are obviously powerful words and conjure up all kinds of inspiring images. They also mean far more to people when they re resent a living covenant as opposed to just being words painted on a wall.

Rick Telander goes on to tell about a massive Wisconsin lineman (6'4", 320 pounds) who at one time perhaps held dreams of a professional career in the National Football League. The account centers on a sports psychologist, who also happens to be a colleague and friend of mine, by the name of Rick Aberman.

As the meeting unfolds between Aberman and the player, it becomes clear that the mental state and attitude of the player is at risk.

The player's perspective of the coaches is something like this: "The coaches' attitudes are so up and down, it's hard for players to stay on an even keel here. Everything changes all the time. Mind games piss me off. I give 100%, so don't jack me around."

A word of caution here: This is not the only environment where this sort of disconnect between high rhetoric and behavior occur. In business, the phrase "walk the talk" speaks to the same issue. My experience in corporate America supports the work of Rick Aberman. *Players and teams need and are thirsting for coaches to be coaches and operate with integrity and authenticity.*

The player in Telander's book, like the second shift employee, is looking to the coach for support, guidance, direction, feedback, and encouragement. They are not seeking manipulation, buzzwords about team, and pep talks that leave little real substance. Rather, they seek coaches who can help raise their game to the next level, to see possibilities that they cannot see clearly for themselves.

When this occurs, the manager as a coach creates practices that ensure a legacy of player/employee development, self-confidence, and high performance with winning attitudes.

These illustrations serve to show what is under the control of a coach in preparation of the team or individual contributor to win at the game of life, business, or any field of endeavor.

Emerson Fittipaldi, famous former race car driver and now consultant, was asked to comment on what he thought made an effective team. His response was very interesting. It was not surprising, given his sport, that he used the Roger Penske Race Team as an example and then went on to say, *"The ability to respond quickly under pressure in the most effective manner makes the difference between winning and losing."*

Coaches, business executives, and team leaders often find themselves asking the same kinds of questions about how to enhance performance. Bill Walsh, former coach of the San Francisco 49ers, believes that high-performance teams and organizations must share a common vision and purpose, which create alignment and cohesion.

The team that acts with unity of purpose has the opportunity to outperform its competition and achieve lasting competitive advantage. However, this state of being purposeful, creating a prevailing championship spirit, doesn't just happen. The price of admission for this performance is the ongoing vigilance by the coach, after creating the mood of hope, aspiration, trust, ambition, success, and competence of team, that this mood is sustainable over time.

As former NFL guru and masterful coach Bill Walsh admits:

In today's environment of player and owner attitude, pressure to win in the short term, moving along to another team when performance is off, and the owners holding the coach responsible, [all this] makes repeating as champions more difficult.

It's worth noticing that development of sustainable competitive advantage takes time and a commitment of resources. There are real parallels to business here as well. A firm may produce record earnings and fantastic overall performance in one year, and then, given a sudden shift in market conditions, customer preferences, and economic factors, it finds itself scrambling to salvage a subpar year.

Turbulence wreaks havoc on the business team, often bringing about cutbacks in training and development budgets, causing key learning opportunities to be shortchanged; then teams tumble. *Have you experienced this scenario in your work environment?*

Under these challenging conditions, what once was exciting, uplifting, inspiring, and attainable now is only a remote possibility. If the team loses its focus and becomes disillusioned, the corresponding performance will produce below-expectation results.

In order to regain the spirit of team, the coach must revisit the vision and purpose of the team and ensure that all team members understand the team purpose and importance of their role and contributions.

Once this step is taken, the individual conversations between coach and employee, associate, or player must happen. Taking this step will avoid the possibility of team members creating their own version or looking at "what's wrong with the team" as an inner conversation. This can be a painful process, like surgery; the only anesthetic is the truth and an honest, direct approach with each player by the coach.

Core elements of this process of preparation are trust, communication, clear performance standards and measures, and a follow-up system with feedback. As you become aware of the stages of team development and knowledgeable in the management of mood, the possibility exists for you to make breakthrough shifts in the minds and hearts of your team members. You become an inspiration for optimal performance.

You can create strategies as a coach that will sustain championship performance over an extended period of time. No strategies are absolutes, but they do become more predictable with practice.

There are options and interpretations that you can bring to your coaching situations to augment and supplement these tactics. Your personal background further enhances your own coaching effectiveness. The critical difference is to *act with integrity and authenticity with others.* Thus, you are seen as sincere in your words and deeds in the eyes of those you are coaching.

The overall result will be more productive coaching relationships, with less hassle for you and those you are coaching, and improved performance. You, the coach, see beyond the immediate task, activity, or goal to the grander "big picture"—the vision of what's possible.

Like all great coaches, your legacy to those you coach can be raising the level of human and team performance to standards not thought possible by those you are coaching. It is within you to help shape the future outcome of those around you, because you are uniquely positioned to inspire greatness.

This, then, is both your greatest gift and greatest challenge: *You hold in your heart and mind the capacity to be the coach and truly soar in a new work environment!*

Maybe you have had a similar experience to this, described to me by a friend of mine who was president of a large food manufacturing division. One of his passions in life was his golf game.

John was committed to making this year the year he reduced his handicap from 17 to 7. He took a first bold step by admitting he needed a coach. John was ready to take instruction. His mental attitude was not one of wanting to show the local pro how good he was, but rather, of remaining open to new learning and coaching.

The coach, after viewing John's stance, approach, grip, swing, and attitude, asked an important question. "John, in order to play the kind of golf you are interested in playing, the best golf you are capable of playing, are you willing to completely take your game apart, to start over to achieve your goal?"

John answered, "Yes."

But, little did he know the power of his response or the implications of what he was agreeing to, for in his response he demonstrated what must happen for you to succeed as a coach and the environment the coach must create in order for coaching to occur. *You must be open to coaching. When you are ready for coaching you are in a position to both hear and act in the present.*

As John learned quite quickly, he found himself frustrated that as he began to change his game, his scores began going up rather than down. Suddenly, instead of hitting greens he was missing them. Where he had been able to drive the ball well off the tee, now he was experiencing a temporary setback to his drive; it was shorter, and less controllable.

There also had been a time when John felt his short game was his strength. Now, as he redefined this area of his game, he learned he could improve here as well.

Over time and with more precise coaching and practice, John had his new game in working order.

Coaching requires regular and ongoing instruction and practice. Thus, the coach prepared John to win, but within the context of what John wanted. The coach saw what was possible and different. He helped John take his game to a higher level, beyond what John saw as possible.

The coach, along with the team or individual players, develops a game plan. The players learn from a playbook. Of course, this is different for the individual competitor in that there are individual moves the player must make in order to win or to position him- or herself to have the possibility of winning. Nonetheless, the principle is the same: It takes preparation, planning, practice, and rehearsal, which must precede the actual game playing or competition in order to have the chance to win. In business I have often experienced a lack of understanding of this principle. Instead, the common occurrence is the proverbial "sink or swim" approach.

It's fair and reasonable to ask, "Why does the sink or swim approach happen so often in business?" While I would not want to make the universal statement that all business is focused on only the financial drivers of the business, generally there is little tolerance for activities that do not add to the bottom line. Frankly, all too often the development and training of human resources are early casualties in the war for cost reduction, fixing the bottom line.

Coaching often falls into the mind-set of "nice to do, but not necessary to do" in business. So, not only do some business organizations fail to invest in, recognize, and address the ongoing need for employee development, they also do not adequately develop their teams.

The classic illustration of the stages of team development by Tuckman clearly describes the four stages of teams' growth and maturity. All teams go through the process of forming, storming, norming, and performing.

In any coaching relationship, the coach and the team must successfully navigate together through times of turbulence, storming and forming, as well as times of cohesion, norming and performing.

The individual coaching relationship might well take on similar shape as well. The business coach might well be advised to pay attention to the various stages of team development.

This landmark research has been used in virtually all management courses as a fundamental model to think about the formulation of stages of team development.

Winning with this concept is more about guiding and facilitating the team through the four stages and truing to a constant vision of what the team aspires to be. Obviously, the coach of the individual contributor must address the individual relationship between coach and coachee as the contributor potentially moves through the four stages of the individual coaching relationship.

This topic alone could well take up an entire book. Suffice it to say that successful coaches of both teams and/or individual contributors must at all times be aware of the stages of those they are coaching. Growth, maturity, development, and readiness must be noticed to offer appropriate coaching. Being aware of this concept and what the coach can do to better position his or her team to thrive in each of the four stages is important.

Refer to the "Scorecard for Team Development" that follows to guide your efforts in coaching as well as being coached. These lists can also be helpful as you coach your team through the stages of team development. Study both the team development stages diagram and the scorecard before you do the Application Exercise.

Scorecard for Team Development

Coach	Team Member
• Remain open.	• Remain open.
• Share vision.	• Be on the team.
• Communicate clearly and often with team.	• Fully participate.
• Create an environment of trust and getting to know each other.	• Learn about teammates.
• Clarify barriers/boundaries.	• Be willing to explore the possible values and beliefs of this team.
• Stay on course; work through turbulence.	• Don't give up.
• Be a role model; employ healthy interpersonal skills.	• Be flexible.
• Clarify expectations.	• Use "I" statements; talk directly to problem sources.
• Create standards, a covenant, and rewards, as well as recognition of consequences of nonconformance.	• Leave out personal agendas.
• Coach both team and individuals to a common purpose.	• Focus on the task.
• Be vulnerable.	• Validate past experience.
•Offer support and encouragement.	• Be a participant, not a spectator.
• Create agreement as to values.	• Support values of the team.
• Focus on "big team, little me."	• Be aware of others' worth.
• Coach when and where appropriate.	• Be part of solution, not just problem.
• Don't be a spectator; support and share glory and success.	• Give 100%.
• Don't overcontrol the team.	• Push yourself.
• Don't compete with individuals, but rather collaborate.	• Enjoy success.
• Inspire the team to next level of performance.	• Celebrate victory; value teammates.

While I have touched on mood management as an internal component of coaching, I would not do justice to this chapter without further highlighting attitude as a driver of performance when preparing the team to win. C. K. Prahalad and Larry Wilson, founder of Wilson Learning, offered me profound insights on the notion of *playing to win versus playing not to lose.*

These two different perspectives about playing the game set up dramatically different moves available to teams and/or individual contributors in their performance. All too often, the mind-set of playing not to lose causes overconservative behavior, aversion to risk, hunkering down, and withdrawal from the action. The results are missed opportunities and ultimately losing.

On the other hand, playing to win causes a different rush of emotion, energy, and persistence. While it is true one can become overzealous in the lust to win, the team and/or individual contributor operating out of this mind-set fosters more of a can-do attitude and finds ways to achieve victory.

Imagine for a moment that some of the great thinkers, explorers, and leaders in history—Christopher Columbus, Martin Luther King Jr., Albert Einstein, Alfred Nobel, George Washington, and Mother Teresa, to name just a few—lived their lives with a playing not to lose mentality.

Now imagine yourself with a playing to win mentality. What's possible for you as a coach? Approaching life with a playing to win attitude allows you access to new moves. What potential barriers to your success now melt away? When you leave behind the playing not to lose thinking and focus on creating success for your team, things move in a different direction. As an individual contributor, a game plan built on possibilities of success brings success!

As a coach, you can create with others a spirit and heartfelt belief in what's possible when they play to win and resist the temptation to play not to lose.

We began our journey together by establishing a business imperative for coaching, highlighting the lightning-quick pace of change in business today. We also made a case that to be world-class, one needs to be more than simply in a position to live with change, but rather, proactively effect change through coaching as a managerial competency.

In the second chapter, we made the point that to be a coach, one needs to accept that a transition must occur in order to successfully move from the old paradigm of just managing things to including coaching competencies. Another way to think about this proposition is moving from cop to coach.

Part of this shift is the idea of bringing your intentionality or the mind-set of *being* a coach to the coaching relationship. You have your self-inventories to assist you in this process. I strongly invite you to use these as a means to more smoothly make the transition through turbulence.

Part of our work in this area was the identification of the skills and behaviors of a coach, as well as the qualities and attributes—and the wisdom to know the difference between them. In addition, you worked on many Application Exercises that enabled you to apply your unique learning and insights from each chapter to your real world of work.

In Chapter 3 we focused on the differences between managing as a good thing to *do*, and a coach as a good thing to *be*, with their unique distinctions. This chapter invited you to examine the differences between *doing things right* and *doing the right things*. I extended you an invitation to examine your world of work and to prioritize those activities that grab your time and attention, directing you toward understanding which are coaching and which are managing. Perhaps there are some activities you might let go of or delegate as a means of focusing on the care and feeding of your people.

In Chapter 4 we addressed the notions of competing priorities and the quick fix. We investigated the romance of "getting it done now" regarding the development of people, even at the risk of shortchanging the real learning. You worked on strategies to overcome this dilemma and created a plan through the Application Exercises to implement your ideas at work.

Chapter 5 identified how we can all get knocked off course in life by turbulence. The challenge is how to get back on track as smoothly and quickly as possible. We asked you to look at your own vulnerabilities and reactions to the turbulence in your life and what you could do to create new possibilities for yourself, thus enabling you to better navigate the turbulence that might come along in coaching.

Nowhere in the book was there a more pivotal moment than in Chapter 6, when "chalking the field"—the process in coaching where the coach and coachee share performance expectations with one another—was introduced. In this part of the coaching relationship standards are set, mutual expectations are shared, desired consequences are established, and the boundaries of the relationship are agreed upon and adhered to. This step to the coaching process is critical; without it, hopes are dashed and disappointment is the product.

Chapter 7 brought us face to face with the power of language, a necessary key to the coaching relationship. Great coaches recognize the opportunity to convey appropriate content and delivery in the coaching message. The mutually decided on commitment and not mere compliance to coaching must be established.

Today, as described in Chapter 8, coaching is not limited to the traditional boss/subordinate relationship. It cuts across peers and team members, and even offers opportunities to "influence up" (coach the boss).

In Chapter 9, we raised the point that world-class athletes train and condition themselves for competition. Why should it be any different for the world of business coaching? We asked the question, "Who coaches the coach?" Your challenge was to continue to improve and enhance your coaching competencies and continuously stretch yourself to grow and learn.

We set the stage in the first nine chapters for the challenge of Chapter 10 and for all coaches: *How do you prepare the team to win?* Part of the answer already lies within you. It's up to you to bring out the best in those you are coaching.

In Chapter 11 you will learn how you can extend your coaching through those you are coaching.

You are already participating in the game of life and work and are becoming a profound contributor as a business coach creating new work environments, because your perspectives have become heightened and you have learned to see in new ways. *What will the record say about you as a coach? Give yourself the time to develop as an authentic coach. You have the power to create the story of you as coach!*

Application Exercise

STATE OF READINESS

The Application Exercise for this chapter is designed to assist you in your efforts to prepare your team or individual contributor to win. As you have with all the other Application Exercises, please be open and candid with yourself about your current situation. Good luck and good coaching! Answer the following questions:

- How ready (not at all, somewhat, very ready) is this team or individual to successfully compete and achieve the assignment, task, or job? Why?

  _____

- What shift in thinking, behavior, and/or competence might be required in order to successfully achieve the assignment, task, or job? _____

  _____

- What stage of team development, or relationship with you, the coach, is the coachee in? What evidence do you see that would support this view? _____

  _____

- Given the current state, what can you do as a coach to cause the necessary shift in thinking, attitude, behavior, or skill development? _____

  _____

- How would you best describe the current mood of the team or individual you are coaching? _____

  _____

• What elements of attitude would you want to:

Build on?_____

_____

Eliminate altogether? _____

_____

Consider reshaping?_____

• What will your coaching game plan include to accomplish this?

CREATING A GAME PLAN

Below are key components of the game plan that you need to prepare before entering the coaching situation. Take the information from the preparation questions above, consider the stages of team development diagram and the scorecard for team development, and complete the following data.

• Name of team, team members, and their stage of development: _____

_____

• What is the vision for the team? _____

_____

• How do I as the coach create alignment from each individual toward the team vision? _____

_____

Ready, set, go! Prepare yourself for your and your team's success. You as the coach will set the tone for the team and each team member. You can greatly impact the current and future lives of those you coach. You have already started you own self-development and are ready for the next level.

11

Overtime
Extending the Possibility of Being a Coach

I was working on a project in southwest Texas when over dinner the following story was related to me.

The town high school enjoyed a long and rich tradition of producing both outstanding young people and contributing citizens—as well as state champion sports teams. This was truly a model "student athlete" school district.

The girls' high school volleyball team had just won the state championship. The team was made up of a group of overachievers rather than having an overabundance of pure volleyball talent. The coach was described as a woman of vision, poise, and confidence, and a winner. She inspired optimum performance from all of her players and collectively from the team. Parents, friends, and the community bubbled with pride in the team's Cinderella season and storybook finish as state champs.

As reported to me by a business client, the decisive factor was the coach's ability to get the absolute best out of each of her players. In the business executive's mind, the coach coached the team to success.

> Following this triumph, those same young women who had won a state championship in volleyball failed to get past a first-round loss in the district basketball tournament and finished last in their conference.

Interestingly, the team not only changed sports, which required a different set of skills, but also changed coaches. *The volleyball coach coached the team, while the basketball coach just managed the team.* The different approaches to coaching had dramatically different effects on the team. Do you believe coaches make a difference?

To the pure sports enthusiasts the reasons were clear: The sports were different, competition was different, the players were tired, there were a few close games that should have been won but weren't, and the players didn't practice the fundamentals well. These were all the *conventional wisdom* reasons that the team failed to reach or exceed expectations. These reasons were all true, and they were also obstacles that any sports team might encounter and must overcome and adjust to.

But, *the most insightful and nonobvious difference in the two teams' successes was in the coaching*!

Here is what makes this story of interest to the business coach.

What are your perspectives as you are becoming a business coach? What do you see when looking at the difference in performance of these same champion women, who only replaced their volleyball uniforms with basketball uniforms? Notice how quickly they fell from grace into the abyss!—a relevant example of what can happen in the business environment.

Remember, we have already established that in business, as in any field, both coaching and managing have their role, place, and unique value. In the game of life, more often than not we do not get a second chance at missed opportunities. However, the business coach, creating a game plan, has the unique potential to extend future success beyond short-term failure through coaching. A lifelong learner, which all great coaches are committed to being, grows through life's setbacks and challenges. Situations, various life scenarios, as well as the speed bumps of life, while disappointing, are overcome and turned into learning opportunities to win the next one. For the coach and those whom he or she is coaching celebrate the small victory, while sustaining themselves on the path of continuous improvement. You are now on the path of developing the critical knowledge, skills, and attitude to be a competent coach in business in the new work environment.

As the great philosopher and wise one, Yoda, told Luke Skywalker, "The Force is within you; it's all around you; it flows through the universe!" Yoda, as coach to young Skywalker, helped prepare him for his development and training as a Jedi warrior. The legacy that Luke inherited from his coach propelled him beyond what he could have seen for himself or accomplished on his own. The coach has the capacity to help release the force that is inside others.

What will your legacy as a coach be? Remember, you are creating the future with others now. What will you help create?

Appendix: The Coach's Playbook

Welcome to the session about the use of the Coach's Playbook. This Playbook offers the business coach the opportunity to capture key learnings from the coaching chapters and translate them into action plans that make sense for your world of work. You will gain the most out of these planning sessions when you apply the Application Exercises from the chapters to the unique challenges you face as a coach on the job and in your daily interactions with those individuals you work with.

Just as a world-class and championship-caliber team creates a set of moves or plays in order to compete, so must you as a business coach design a set of moves or plays that will enable you to compete in new work environments. In the world of theater and motion pictures, the director must prepare the cast to perform the play or film. It is your role and task as a business coach to prepare the business team to win.

A critical first step in the process is your own individual preparation and readiness to coach.

This Coach's Playbook will assist you in this process. Complete each "play" in sequence before going onto the next. By doing this, you will be creating a total game plan first. Then you will go back, refining and adjusting as needed. The opportunity to see the entire playing field, while at the same time being aware of your team members, will give you the resources needed to accomplish your plan.

The framework by which you create the game plan is here. You bring your uniqueness, adapting it to your individual style and personal interests. Feel free to tailor or customize the process to achieve your goals, while at the same time staying aware of not shortcutting the plan. The benefit for you and those you wish to coach will be significant as you attend to the ongoing work of updating and recreating the plan and developing the plays as it makes sense to do so.

The intent of the Coach's Playbook is to provide you as a coach with a real-time tool that can be accessed and used on a consistent basis to assist you in your coaching. Good luck as a coach, and much continued success!

PLAY #1

My current key result areas (KRAs) for the year include:

PLAY #2

The team I am currently coaching includes:

Name	Position	Key Strength	Key Developmental Goal

PLAY #3

Key initiatives the team is working on include:

PLAY #4

Key barriers, obstacles, or issues I see for the team's success include:

PLAY #5

Key resources needed for the team's success include:

PLAY #6

My coaching game plan for the success of the team and accomplishments for each KRA include:

KRA Initiative	Planning Needed	Action Taken	Follow-Up Work

PLAY #7

What are the measurements or scorecard that will monitor and track KRAs for myself the team?

KRA	Team Member	Measurement Criterion	Score	Next Step for Follow-Up

PLAY #8

What key learning as a coach will help me in the accomplishment of my game plan?

PLAY #9

What new knowledge, skills, and attitudes might I continue to acquire to improve my coaching?

Knowledge:

Skills:

Attitudes:

PLAY #10

What practice(s) might I design for myself that will engage me to grow and develop as a coach?

What could I do each day or week to work on my new target knowledge, skills, and attitudes?

How can I measure my progress?

What do I need to change or adjust to impact the above?

Behaviors:

Actions:

Thinking:

How can I reward myself or give myself recognition for my efforts and success in my coaching?

PLAY #11

What is my current mood and belief about coaching?

What might I do to continue to be aware of how my own intentionality enhances my coaching?

What daily "self-talk" affects my thinking and behavior as a coach?

PLAY #12

Who could I enlist, ask for help, and seek out as my coach? Who would give me ongoing support, feedback, and encouragement? What competency could this person help me develop and fine-tune?

Name	Relationship	Areas of Competence

PLAY #13

Are there any other additional inputs or areas of development I might consider that would enhance my ongoing development as a coach?

Supplemental Reading

Beckhand, Richard, and Pritchard, Wendy. *Changing the Essence: The Art of Creating and Leading Fudamental Change in Organizations*. San Francisco: Jossey-Bass Publishers, 1987.

Bennett, Robert F. *Gaining Control: Your Key to Freedom and Success*. Salt Lake City: Franklin Institute, Inc., 1987.

Bennis, Warren. *On Becoming a Leader*. Reading, MA: Addison-Wesley Publishing Company, Inc., 1989.

Blatherwick, Jack. *Overspeed—Skill Training for Hockey*. Colorado Springs: USA Hockey, 1992.

Bracey, Hyler; Rosenblum, Jack; Sandford, Aubney; and Trueblood, Roy. *Managing from the Heart*. New York: Bantam Doubleday Dell Publishing Group, Inc., 1990.

Bridges, William. *Managing Transitions: Making the Most of Change*. Reading, MA: Addison-Wesley Publishing Company, Inc., 1993.

Chopra, Deepak, M.D. *Ageless Body, Timeless Mind: The Quantum Alternative to Growing Old*. New York: Harmony Books, 1993.

Collins, James C., and Porras, Jerry I. *Built to Last: Successful Habits of Visionary Companies*. New York: HarperCollins Publishers, 1994.

Covey, Stephen R. *The Seven Habits of Highly Effective People*. New York: Simon & Schuster, 1989.

Eliot, Robert S., M.D. *Is It Worth Dying For? A Self-Assessment Program to Make Stress Work for You, Not Against You.* New York: Bantam Books, 1984.

Fournies, Ferdinand F. *Coaching for Improved Work Performance.* New York: Van Nostrand Reinhold Company, 1978.

Frankl, Viktor E. *Man's Search for Meaning.* Boston: Beacon Press, 1959.

Garfield, Charles. *Peak Performers: The New Heroes of American Business.* New York: Avon Books, 1986.

Kriegel, Robert J., and Patler, Louis. *If It Ain't Broke . . . Break It! And Other Unconventional Wisdom for a Changing Business World.* New York: Warner Books, 1991.

Larsen, Earnie, and Goodstein, Jeanette. *Who's Driving Your Bus?* San Diego: Pfieffer & Company, 1993.

Leonard, George. *Mastery: The Keys to Long-Term Success and Fulfillment.* New York: Plume: Penguin Group, 1982.

McCallister, Linda. *I Wish I'd Said That! How to Talk Your Way Out of Trouble and into Success.* New York: John Wiley & Sons, Inc., 1992.

McNally, David. *Even Eagles Need a Push: Learning to Soar in a Changing World.* Shorewood, MN: Trans-Form Press, 1990.

Massnick, Forler. *The Customer Is CEO.* New York: AMACOM, 1997.

Nhat Hanh, Thich. *Call Me by My True Names.* Berkeley: Parallax Press, 1993.

Peck, M. Scott, M.D. *The Road Less Traveled: A New Psychology of Love, Traditional Values and Spiritual Growth.* New York: Simon & Schuster, 1994.

Riley, Pat. *The Winner Within: A Life Plan for Team Players.* New York: G. P. Putnam's Sons, 1993.

Shula, Don, and Blanchard, Ken. *Everyone's a Coach: You Can Inspire Anyone to Be a Winner.* Grand Rapids, MI: Zondervan, 1995.

Stonell, Steven J., and Starcevich, Matt M. *The Coach: Creating Partnerships for a Competitive Edge.* Salt Lake City: The Center for Management and Organization Effectiveness, 1987.

Telander, Rick. *From Red Ink to Roses: The Turbulant Transformation of a Big Ten Program.* New York: Simon & Schuster, 1994.

Trungpa, Chögyam. *Shambhala: The Sacred Path of the Warrior.* Boston and London: Shambhala, 1988.

Index